THE BAFFLER

W9-AZL-064

SPRING 2001 NUMBER 14

TABLE OF CONTENTS

The BAFFLER

Editor
Thomas Frank

Managing Editor
"Diamonds" Dave Mulcahey

Associate Editors
Michael Szalay, Matt Weiland

Fiction Editor
Gwenan Wilbur

Poetry Editor
Jennifer Moxley

Publisher
Greg Lane

Associate Publisher
Emily Vogt

Founders
Thomas Frank, Keith White

Contributing Editors
**Kim Phillips-Fein,
Christy MacLemahan**

Hodaktion
George Hodak

Subscriptions to THE BAFFLER cost $24 for four issues and can be purchased by check at the address below, or by credit card at thebaffler.com and 1-888-387-8947. The editors invite submissions of art, fiction, and essays. Unsolicited poetry submissions will not be considered or returned. All submissions must be accompanied by a stamped, addressed envelope. Submissions should be addressed to the Editor and not to individuals. Unsolicited manuscripts not accompanied by stamped and addressed envelopes will not be returned and the Editors will not enter into correspondence about them. All contributions are paid for on acceptance, without reference to the date of publication. All requests for permissions and reprints must be made in writing to the Publisher. Six weeks advance notice is required for changes of address.

THE BAFFLER is printed in the United States. All correspondence should be sent to the address below.

We sent this issue of THE BAFFLER safely to the printer on April 11, 2001.

On April 25, years of incendiary cultural criticism finally achieved ignition. A pre-dawn fire swept through our office, awakening residents of Chicago's South Side to the unmistakable smell of burning BAFFLERS. As page after charred page lofted heavenward in a plume of black smoke, we reflected on the grim prescience of Hunter Kennedy's cover art for issue 13 ("In Flames!"). And as fire hoses turned box upon box of back issues into so much prose pulp, we began to calculate the magnitude of the disaster.

Our loss was enormous and recovery will be difficult. For those who can help financially, send checks to The Baffler Recovery Fund at the P.O. Box below. For detailed information about donations, go to thebaffler.com, write us, or email fire@thebaffler.com.

THE BAFFLER wishes to thank Dan Peterman and Connie Spreen, who built and will rebuild. Also: Dan Raeburn, Solveig Nelson, Jake Spicer, Sarah Ward, Deanna Bradley, Eric Shutt, Patrick Welch (for extraordinary physical exertions), Wendy Edelberg, Jim Skish, Donny Gillen and the brave men of the Chicago Fire Department, Tuli Kupferberg (for "The Peacemaker"), Kate Shanks, Bill Ayers, Bruce Johnstone, Mike Herwitt the Carpenter, Dave Gantz the Mason, Tom Brock the Architect, Paul Maliszewski, Josh Glenn, Rick MacArthur, Studs Terkel, André Schiffrin, Serge Halimi, Brad Kotler, Sarah Reis, Jack Guthman, Jim Wilson, Stephanie Smith and Kimerly Rorschach from the Smart Museum, Greg Sholette, Francisco Caudet, Katie and Tim at the Hideout, John Corbett and Terri Kapsalis and all at the Empty Bottle, Dwayne Brown, Ray McDaniel of Shaman Drum, Barbara Kennen and Lois Weisberg of the Chicago Department of Cultural Affairs, the crew of 6100 Blackstone, all our friends who pulled guard duty there, donned some work gloves, or brought coffee, food, or liquor. A long and growing list of people have donated money, service, and sympathy. Among them are our fellows at *Harper's*, the *Nation*, the *Industry Standard*, *Hermenaut*, *McSweeney's*, and *Bridge*.

P.O. Box 378293, Chicago, Ills. 60637 · thebaffler.com

THE GOD THAT SUCKED

Thomas Frank

Despite this, many economists still think that electricity deregulation will work. A product is a product, they say, and competition always works better than state control.

"I believe in that premise as a matter of religious faith," said Philip J. Romero, dean of the business school at the University of Oregon and one of the architects of California's deregulation plan.

—New York Times, *February 4, 2001*

TIME WAS, the only place a guy could expound the mumbo jumbo of the free market was in the country club locker room or the pages of *Reader's Digest*. Spout off about it anywhere else and you'd be taken for a Bircher or some new strain of Jehovah's Witness. After all, in the America of 1968, when the great backlash began, the average citizen, whether housewife or hardhat or salary-man, still had an all-too-vivid recollection of the Depression. Not to mention a fairly clear understanding of what social class was all about. Pushing laissez-faire ideology back then had all the prestige and credibility of hosting a Tupperware party.

But thirty-odd years of culture war have changed all that. Mention "elites" these days and nobody thinks of factory owners or gated-community dwellers. Instead they assume that what you're mad as hell about is the liberal media, or the pro-criminal judiciary, or the tenured radicals, or the know-it-all bureaucrats.

For the guys down at the country club all these inverted forms of class war worked spectacularly well. This is not to say that the right-wing culture warriors ever out-smarted the liberal college professors or shut down the Hollywood studios or re-pealed rock 'n' roll. Shout though they might, they never quite got cultural history to stop. But what they did win was far more important: political power, a free hand to turn back the clock on such non-glamorous issues as welfare, taxes, OSHA, even the bankruptcy laws, for chrissake. Assuring their millionaire clients that culture war got the deregulatory job done, they simply averted their eyes as bizarre backlash variants flowered in the burned-over districts of conserva-tism: Posses Comitatus, backyard Con-federacies mounting mini-secessions, crusades against Darwin.

For most of the duration of the thirty-year backlash, the free-market faiths of the economists and the bosses were kept discreetly in the background. To be sure, market worship was always the established church in the halls of Republican power, but in public the chant was usually *States' Rights,* or *Down with Big Gummint,* or *Watch out for Commies,* or *Speak English Goddammit.* All Power to the Markets has never been too persuasive as a rallying cry.

So confidently did the right proceed from triumph to triumph, though, that eventually they forgot this. Inspired by a generous bull market and puffed up by a sense of historical righteousness so cocksure that it might have been lifted from *The God That Failed,* that old book in which ex-Communists disavowed their former convictions, the right evidently decided in the Nineties that the time had come to tell the world about the wonders of the market.

D INESH D'SOUZA, pedagogical product of the Jesuits, these days can be found swinging the censer for Mammon and thrilling to the mayhem his ruthless "god of the market" visits on the undeserving poor. George Gilder, erstwhile elder of the Christian right, is now the Thirty-Third Degree Poobah in the Temple of Telecosm, where he channels the libertarian commandments of his digital Juggernaut in the language of the angels.

A host of awesome myths attest to the power of this new god. Markets must rule, some right-wing prophets tell us, because of "globalization," because the moral weight of the entire world somehow demands it. Others bear tidings of a "New Economy," a spontaneous recombination of the DNA of social life according to which, again, markets simply must rule. The papers fill with

rapturous talk of historical corners turned, of old structures abandoned, of endless booms and weightless work.

The new god makes great demands on us, and its demands must be appeased. None can be shielded from its will. The welfare of AFDC mothers must be entrusted unhesitatingly to its mercies. Workers of every description must learn its discipline, must sacrifice all to achieve flexibility, to create shareholder value. The professional, the intellectual, the manager must each shed their pride and own up to their flawed, lowly natures, must acknowledge their impotence and insensibility before its divine logic. We put our health care system in its invisible hands, and to all appearances it botches the job. Yet the faith of the believers is not shaken. We deregulate the banking industry. Deregulate the broadcasters. Deregulate electricity. Halt antitrust. Make plans to privatize Social Security and to privatize the public schools.

And to those who worry about the cost of all this, the market's disciples speak of mutual funds, of IPOs, of online trading, of early retirement. All we have to do is believe, take our little pile of treasure down to the god's house on Wall Street, and the market rewards us with riches undreamed of in human history. It gives us a Nasdaq that is the envy of the world and a 401(K) for each of us to call his own.

Then, one fine day, you check in at Ameritrade and find that your tech portfolio is off 90 percent. Your department at work has been right-sized, meaning you spend a lot more time at the office— without getting a raise. You have one kid in college to the tune of $30,000 a year, another with no health insurance because she's working as a temp. Or maybe you lost your job because they can do it cheaper in Alabama or Mexico. Your daughter's got a disease that requires $400 a month in drugs, and your COBRA insurance benefits are due to run out in two months. Or maybe you're the Mexican worker who just got a new maquiladora job. You have no electricity, no running water, no school for your children, no health care, and your wage is below subsistence level. And should you make any effort to change these conditions—say, by organizing a union not aligned with the corrupt PRI—you're likely to get blacklisted by local factory managers.

That's when it dawns on you: The market is a god that sucks. Yes, it cashed a few out at the tippy top, piled up the loot of the world at their feet, delivered shiny Lexuses into the driveways of their ten-bedroom suburban chateaux. But for the rest of us the very principles that make the market the object of D'Souza's worship, of Gilder's awestruck piety, are the forces that conspire to make life shitty in a million ways great and small. The market is the reason our housing is so expensive. It is the reason our public transportation is lousy. It is the reason our cities sprawl idiotically all across the map. It is the reason our word processing programs stink and our prescription drugs cost more than anywhere else. In order that a fortunate few might enjoy a kind of prosperity unequaled in human history, the rest of us have had to abandon ourselves to a lifetime of casual employment, to unquestioning obedience within an ever-more arbitrary and despotic corporate regime, to medical care available on a maybe/maybe-not basis, to a housing market interested in catering only to the fortunate. In order for the libertarians of Orange County to enjoy the smug sleep of the true believer, the thirty millions among whom they live must join them in the dark.

BUT IT IS NOT enough to count the ways in which the market sucks. This is a deity of spectacular theological agility, supported by a priesthood of millions: journalists, admen, politicians, Op-Ed writers, think-tankers, cyberspace scrawlers, Sunday morning talk-show libertarians, and, of course, bosses, all of them united in the conviction that, no matter what, the market can't be held responsible. When things go wrong only we are to blame. After all, they remind us, every step in the economic process is a matter of choice. We choose Ford over Dodge and Colgate Total over Colgate Ultra-Whitening; we choose to take that temp job at Microsoft, to live in those suburbs, to watch Channel 4 rather than Channel 5. We participate in markets; we build markets; markets, in fact, are us. Markets are a straightforward expression of the popular will. Since markets are the product of our choices, we have essentially authorized whatever the market does to us. This is the world that we have made, let us rejoice and be glad in it.

Virtually any deed can be excused by this logic. The stock market, in recent years a scene of no small amount of deceit, misinformation, and manipulation, can be made to seem quite benign when the high priests roll up their sleeves. In October 1999, a heady time for small investors, Andy Serwer of *Fortune* could be heard telling the inspiring story of an in-

vestment "revolution" in which the financial power of "a few thousand white
males" in New York was "being seized by
Everyman and Everywoman." We the
people had great, unquestionable power:
Serwer's article was even illustrated with
clenched fists. We had built this market,
and it was rewarding us accordingly.

But these days Serwer is pondering the
problem of "stock market rage" as those
same Everyman investors are turned inside out by the destruction of $4 trillion
of Nasdaq value. Now that the country is
in the sort of situation where brokers and
bankers might find themselves in deep
political shit, Serwer observes that we
have become quite powerless. Investors
are "mad as hell," Serwer notes, but "there
isn't much [they] can do about it." The explanation for this supposed impotence is,
strangely, a moral one: Choice. Since
those lovable little guys acted of their own
free will when they invested in Lucent,
PMC Sierra, and Cisco, today there is no
claim they can make that deserves a hearing. What has happened is their fault and
theirs alone.

The market only fails us, it seems,
when we fail it—when our piety is somehow incomplete, when we don't give the
market enough power, when we balk at
entrusting it with our last dime. Electricity deregulation didn't work in California,
the true believers chant, because the
scheming elitist political class of that state
betrayed the people, refusing to give them
enough choice, to deregulate all the way.

F REE TO CHOOSE is a painfully ironic
slogan for the market order. While
markets do indeed sometimes provide a
great array of consumer choices, the clear

intention of much of the chatter about
technology, "globalization," and the "New
Economy" is, in fact, to deny us any choice
at all. Moving from rhetoric to the world
of financial politics the same logic holds
true: Markets show a clear preference for
the shutting down of intellectual dissent
and political choice. Markets romp joy-
fully when word arrives that the vote-
counting has been halted. Markets pun-
ish the bond prices of countries where
substantial left parties still flourish. Markets reward those lands—like Bill Clinton's
USA—where left parties have been trian-
gulated into impotence. So predictably do
markets celebrate the suppression of political difference that Thomas Friedman,
the highly respected *New York Times* columnist, has actually come up with a term
for the trade-off: "the golden straitjacket."
Since all alternatives to laissez-faire are
now historically discredited, Friedman
maintains, all countries must now adopt
the same rigidly pro-business stance.
When they do, "your economy grows
and your politics shrink." The pseudo-
democracy of markets replaces the real
democracy of democracy; the great mul-
tinational corporations nod their approval; and the way is clear for (some)
people to get fantastically rich.

Friedman has a point. Consider the
case of Singapore, long the inamorata of
market heavies and their press agents. As

we all know by now, Singapore is an economic miracle, a land arisen from Third World to First in a handful of decades. Singapore is the land with the most economic freedom in the world. Singapore is more comprehensively wired than anywhere else. Singapore is the best place to do business in all the earth. And as proof you need look no further than a postcard of Singapore's glittering downtown, at all the spanking new skyscrapers erupting from the earth in stern testimony to the market's approval.

And what the market loves best about Singapore is what is absent: Politics. Singapore's shopping malls—heavenly landscapes of chrome and polished granite, of flashing jumbotrons and free floor shows for the kids—trump those of our own land. But politically the country is a dull monotone. Here there is little danger that opposition parties will come to power or that crusading journalists will violate the rules of what Singaporeans call "self-censorship."

So what replaces politics? What fills the blank space left when a country has sacrificed dissent on the altar of the market? In Singapore, the answer seems to be management theory. Settling down one Sunday afternoon in that country with a copy of the *Straits-Times*, the more or less official newspaper, I turned to the section most American newspapers reserve for book reviews and think-pieces and found instead: a profile of the management guru who co-wrote the *One to One* series of marketing books; a column about the urgent need to adapt to waves of workplace "change" (you know, like "outsourcing"); an enthusiastic story about the new president of PepsiCo, a native of

India who reportedly studies videotapes of Michael Jordan's greatest basketball moments in order to "catch insights about the value of teamwork"; a profile of the management guru who co-wrote *The Individualized Corporation* ("Power to the people is [his] motto"); a profile of one of the paper's writers in which the concept of "the journalist as a brand" is the point of departure; and a review of one of those sweeping, pseudo-historical books so beloved of business readers that start out with the Neanderthals and end up affirming various contemporary management homilies about creativity and entrepreneurship.

Management theory has become so variegated in recent years that, for some, it now constitutes a perfectly viable replacement for old-fashioned intellectual life. There's so much to choose from! So many deep thinkers, so many flashy popularizers, so many schools of thought, so many bold predictions, so many controversies!

For all this vast and sparkling intellectual production, though, we hear surprisingly little about what it's like to *be managed*. Perhaps the reason for this is because, when viewed from below, all the glittering, dazzling theories of management seem to come down to the same ugly thing. This is the lesson that Barbara Ehrenreich learns from the series of low-wage jobs that she works and then describes in all their bitter detail in her new book, *Nickel and Dimed*. Pious chatter about "free agents" and "empowered workers" may illuminate the covers of *Fast Company* and *Business 2.0*, but what strikes one most forcefully about the world of waitresses, maids, and Wal-Mart workers that Ehrenreich enters is the overwhelming power of management, the intimidating array of advantages it holds in its endless war on wages. This is a place where even jobs like housecleaning have been Taylorized to extract maximum output from workers ("You know, all this was figured out with a stopwatch," Ehrenreich is told by a proud manager at a maid service), where omnipresent personality and drug tests screen out those of assertive nature, where even the lowliest of employees are overseen by professional-grade hierarchs who crack the whip without remorse or relent, where workers are cautioned against "stealing time" from their employer by thinking about anything other than their immediate task, and where every bit of legal, moral, psychological, and anthropological guile available to advanced civilization is deployed to prevent the problem of pay from ever impeding the upward curve of profitability. This is the real story of life under markets.

But the point where all the "New Economy" glory and promise really start to suck, where all the vaunted choice and empowerment of free markets are revealed as so many creaking stage devices, is when Ehrenreich takes on the shiniest of all the Nineties myths—productivity. With the country as close to full employment as it has ever been in 1999 and 2000, wages did not increase as much as standard economic theory held they ought. Among the devout this was cause for great rejoicing: Through a titanic national effort we had detached productivity from wages, handing the gains over to owners and shareholders instead. But this was less a "choice" that Americans consciously made than it was, as Ehrenreich makes undeniably evident, the simple triumph of the nation's managers, always encouraging employees to think of themselves as stakeholders or team members even as they unilaterally dictate every aspect of the work experience.

The social panorama that Ehrenreich describes should stand as an eternal shrine to the god that sucked: Slum housing that is only affordable if workers take on two jobs at once; exhausted maids eating packages of hot-dog buns for their meals; women in their twenties so enfeebled by this regimen that they can no longer lift the vacuum cleaners that the maid service demands they carry about on their backs; purse searches, drug tests, personality tests, corporate pep rallies. Were we not so determined to worship the market and its boogie-boarding billionaires, Ehrenreich suggests, we might even view their desperate, spent employees as philanthropists of a sort, giving selflessly of their well-being so that the comfortable might live even more comfortably. "They neglect their own children so that the children of others will be cared for," she writes; "they live in substandard housing so that other homes will be shiny and perfect; they endure privation so that inflation will be low and stock prices high."

These are the fruits of thirty years of culture war. Hell-bent to get government off our backs, you installed a tyrant infinitely better equipped to suck the joy out of life. Cuckoo to get God back in the schools, you enshrined a god of unappeasable malice. Raging against the snobs, you enthroned a rum bunch of two-fisted boodlers, upper-class twits, and hang-em-high moralists. Ain't irony grand.

THE ROD OF CORRECTION
Clive Thompson

Cold Warrior in a Cold Country

CANADA HAS NEVER been a hospitable land for right-wingers. Even so, 1991 was a low point for the country's long-frustrated friends of wealth and established power. Unemployment had soared to almost 11 percent, putting an already well-organized union movement on the offensive. A public sector strike was raging, with workers campaigning against a wage freeze. Toronto's public transit employees followed suit, tying the city up in traffic jams. To make matters worse, Ontario had just elected a nakedly left-wing party to run the province—the New Democrats, a tax-and-spend gang headed by one of those fey, bookish elites so loathed by the right.

A bleak spectacle indeed—particularly for Conrad Black, Canada's expatriate media baron. In the Canadian daily business paper the *Financial Post*, he surveyed his home and native land and offered a scathing prognosis. "Only in Canada, especially in Ontario, are the prig stormtroopers of the old, soft, anti-capitalist left still taken seriously when they insolently strive to communize industry, confiscate wealth, and discourage eco-

nomic growth," he railed. "Only in Ontario in the entire democratic world, is the cant and hypocrisy of union-dominated soak-the-rich, anti-productivity, politics of envy officially approved and po-facedly presented as 'caring and compassion.'" Worse, he moaned, the best and brightest Canadians, "demoralized by the socialist quagmire," were fleeing to the *United States*.

After a few more desultory stabs at Canada's tweedy left (alternately described as "simpering" and "driveling") Black came to the meat of the matter: What Canada needed, dammit, was a dose of hard-assed American-style values. It needed tax cuts, more tax cuts, and union busting. Black fondly recalled Reagan's and Nixon's legendary beatdowns of the air-traffic controllers and postal workers. It was, he concluded, really quite simple. Canada needed a culture war, a massive backlash of the kind that had propelled his American heroes—and, indeed, the world—into the age of the market.

Only one niggling problem remained: How could the simpering, driveling Canadians be made to see the light?

With a national newspaper, that's how. Before long, Black launched the *National*

Clive Thompson is a simpering, driveling, po-faced writer in New York.

Post—one of the most aggressive, not to mention expensive, backlash vehicles in Canadian history. From its debut on October 27, 1998, the daily has delivered a virtually non-stop harangue against taxes and organized labor. Many newspapers reflect their owners' viewpoints, of course; but the *National Post* is so thoroughly choked with free-market zealotry that it appears at times to have been written entirely by Black himself, then faxed directly to stunned readers in Moose Jaw or Saskatoon. I'm exaggerating, but only just: Black is, after all, renowned for calling up reporters at some of his most obscure daily papers and dressing them down for false consciousness—as he recently did at the *Montreal Gazette*, bawling out a hack who had dared to criticize his concentrated control of Canada's media.

And so it goes with the *Post*. Day in, day out, the paper adheres religiously to Black's prime directive: Canadians must either pander to the rich, else watch them flee to the risk-and-reward empyrean of the United States or some other tax haven even further afield. "The yacht clubs in the Caribbean and the slopes of Switzerland are filled with wealthy Canadians who will never pay a penny of taxes here, or anywhere else, again," as one columnist scolded. And it's not just the rich who are fed up! An even more important actor in the make-believe world of Blackian theory is the mad-as-hell middle class, who just aren't going to take it anymore. To read the *National Post* one would believe there is a virtual tsunami of "tax rage" sweeping the country, turning average Canadians into "tax rebels"—refusing to pay up and preparing to hunker down with cans of tuna to await the jackbooted

Mounties. "When a nation's citizens are backed against a wall and have little left to lose, they take desperate measures," admonishes *Post* tax columnist Jonathan Chevreau. Black even began using the *Post* to distribute copies of *The Wealthy Boomer*, an anti-tax magazine whose title—despite its viciously populist, down-with-elites content—is just about the most obnoxious bit of class boasting imaginable. (Okay, calling it *The Contented Yuppie* would have been worse.) Meanwhile, a "special report" in a February 1999 *Post* devoted entirely to the anti-tax movement offered glowing profiles of marginal tax-rebel groups, musings about Laffer-curve economic theory, and polls categorizing different sectors of the Canadian public as "high rage" or "medium rage."

The really weird thing about Black, though, is that he himself can't really turn on the populist vibe. Quite the contrary; he harbors some very pronounced aristocratic pretensions. For years, Black has lobbied desperately for admittance to—get this—the British House of Lords, bending himself backward in sucking up to the most calcified symbol of class hierarchy in existence. Last year, Black even went so far as to enlist Tony Blair's aid in an eleventh-hour bid to snag a peerage. Unfortunately, the plan fell afoul of a Canadian government policy prohibiting citizens from accepting honorary titles that "confer any precedence or privilege." When the government told Black he couldn't don an ermine robe in the Sceptr'd Isle, he immediately went apeshit and phoned the Prime Minister to complain. The impudence! The arrogance! The leftism!

Granted, Black has picked his victim well. If you're going to stage a Nixonian freak-out about socialism today, Canada is one of the few places you can still do so without seeming utterly bonkers. It remains an oddly left-wing place in subtle ways and—all the worse for Conrad Black—those ways tend to be the national characteristics most cherished by Canadians themselves. As the Canadian political theorist Gad Horowitz has argued, the country's cultural DNA includes a powerful strand of early British trade unionism, mixed with a lot of union-positive European immigrants. This is not a free-market crowd. The idea of communally pooling money to pay for stuff like health care is the bedrock of the Canadian psyche, not some elitist nostrum imposed from on high by trip-hopping tenured radicals. Canada's would-be backlash warriors are left slightly unsure of who precisely to attack, which is why the *Post* frequently seems to be flailing at anything. Worse, invocations of the glories of American life are instantly derailed by the fact that Canadians, living right next to the United States, have seen enough hair-raising stuff to realize that *Beverly Hills 90210* and *Friends* don't quite reflect the real state of everyday America, with its medically uninsured middle class and crumbling public education system. Yeah, sure, it'd be nice if we never had to pay taxes, everyone figures—*but who wants to end up like Detroit?* This quaint xenophobia powers more Canadian politics than you'd imagine, which is why endless surveys and polls have found that, the *Post's* jihad to the contrary, few Canadians are stirred by Black's dream of massive tax cuts. One study by Ekos Research even shows that anti-tax sentiment has been *falling* ever since 1977.

This is what has made Conrad Black's great cultural experiment so intriguing to watch: It's almost psychotically divorced from everyday Canadian reality. Ordinarily, even the most deformed backlash politics arise out of some bitter claim of injustice inflicted on the *hoi polloi*, some smoldering sense of being hard done by. Since no such anger really exists in Canada, it leaves the *Post's* hapless reporters forced to holographically create their own revolt, spinning isolated cases (here, a shopkeeper who decides to stop paying taxes; there, a bug-eyed letter to the editor) into a full-on "rebellion." Meanwhile, the paper's editors feebly protest that what they're doing isn't cravenly serving the ideological (and financial) wishes of their rich-as-Croesus boss; they're "crusading," in old-skool newspaperman style, trying to wake up the country's somnambulant public. At its best, the paper can be a lively, British-style read; anyway, it's always fun to read a paper that actually comes clean about its ideology. But at its worst, the *Post*'s screeds seem simply hallucinatory, directed to the citizens of an alternate universe who lie awake at night, fretting over whether "taxation is legal." Who *are* these people?

Albertans, possibly. Alberta, being soaked in oil and cowboy culture, comes the closest of any region in Canada to producing Texas-style riches, and thus Texas-style right-wing fervor. Black adroitly realized this, and appointed a young Albertan, Ken Whyte, as his editor in chief. Under Whyte's guidance, the newspaper has devoted seas of ink to Western concerns, under the assumption that they will metastasize and eventually consume the entire country. This technique can at times work fairly well; even the most po-faced, envious, driveling Toronto intellectual will acknowledge that the West probably has some ideas worth considering about how to run things. Hell, those Albertans are still *Canadians*, aren't they? Quite, old chap, quite. And many credit the *Post* with single-handedly creating the new right-wing Western protest party, the Canadian Alliance, by running an endless stream of boosterish stories about its members.

But with Western suspicion of taxes has come the Western mania for family values—including ranting denunciations of feminists and other modern-day witches. From day one Whyte has waged a tireless crusade against women's issues. Reporters have argued that pay equity distorts the market (Headline: "Courts in grip of radical feminism"); that boys are subject to rampant discrimination ("It's a bad time to be a boy"); and that battered women are ... kind of *asking for it*, ain't they? ("Spinning the spousal abuse story"). Indeed, perhaps even more than its anti-tax crusade, the *Post*'s rabid antifeminism decisively removes the paper from the Canadian political orbit, and sends it spinning off somewhere not too far from the moon, or perhaps Pat Robertson.

It is the final irony of Black's project in Canada: For a guy so convinced that free markets will sort everything out, the *Post* has the centrally planned feel of a North Korean government newspaper. And such is Black's mania that he has poured millions into keeping the paper going, even as it geysers red ink. If there's a market for American-style rage in Canada, he hasn't found it.

In fact, he's packing up his tent and leaving. In August 2000, Black announced that he was selling his Canadian newspapers—including fifty percent of the *National Post*—to a Canadian TV mogul named Izzy Asper. Asper is not only considerably more liberal than Black, he's actually a Liberal, having spent a five-year stint as leader of the Liberal Party in Manitoba, a province renowned for left-wing rule. He may have abandoned his homeland to the socialist quagmire, but hopefully there is a happy ending in store for Black himself. Maybe all this will finally clear the way for his admission to the House of Lords, where he can rage and vituperate on behalf of the world's long-suffering rich to a more sympathetic audience.

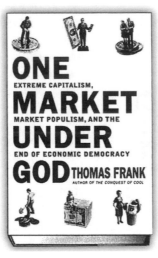

THE EARL BUTZ FARM

ALBION, INDIANA

Michael Martone

EXCEPT FOR the interpretive center in the trailer of a North American moving van, the Earl Butz Farm, the boyhood home of Earl Butz, secretary of agriculture under Richard Nixon, is now part of a larger, privately owned farm. The land itself, four hundred acres in Sycamore Township, is currently owned by an Italian insurance company and is leased to the Big Mac Management Group, a subsidiary of Central Soya Industries of Decatur, Illinois. None of the buildings known to exist during the former secretary's childhood (two houses, summer kitchen, root cellar, storm cellar, mow barn and silo, tool shed, tractor shed, corncrib, coops, pole barns, pumphouse, springhouse, horse barn, grain bins, garages, green houses, mill, machine shop, manure tanks, cannery, warehouse, fuel bunker, loafing shed, pigpens, nursery and farrowing houses, child's play house, woodshed, and outhouse) survives. Before the land is planted, it is possible, with a bit of imagination, to reconstruct the bare outlines of the domestic structures' footprint by using the small stands of rhubarb and horseradish that somehow germinate each year to outline the buildings' lost foundations. One may easily discern the remains of the former dirt-floored basketball court bordered by foxtail and milkweed. There are the ruined and rusted struts of a windmill tower, the well beneath it being too deep to fill, that serve as a base station for the Citizen's Band radio employed by the seasonal field hands. There is not a fence nor fence post in sight, though the interpretive center has a collection of barbed wire. The fertile family graveyard, however, still yields, after all these years, a rich assortment of artifacts and human remains, which are freshly turned up each spring by state-of-the-art mold board chisel plows. Agronomy experts from Purdue University believe that such material will continue to be produced for, perhaps, several years more as the topsoil is routinely eroded. 🖝

Michael Martone is the author of *The Blue Guide to Indiana*, from which this is excerpted. *Flatness and Other Landscapes*, his recent book of essays, won the AWP Award for Nonfiction. He lives in Tuscaloosa, Alabama.

A NEW YORK TIMES NOTABLE BOOK
A LOS ANGELES TIMES BEST BOOK OF 2000

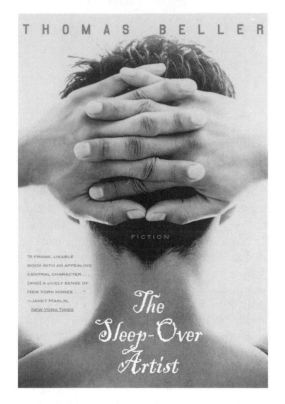

"Hilarious... Beller captures perfectly the myriad stages of fear, discovery, and elation, that mark one's first sexual experience."
—Katherine Deickman, *The New York Times Book Review*

"Featuring a New York that, like Kundera's Prague, is a vast hive of seductions and betrayals, Beller's carefully crafted debut novel (is)... a moving portrait of a young man intuitively seeking a place he can call home."
—*Publishers Weekly*

"Detail and emotion are rendered with astonishing precision and clarity... Readers of Carver and Roth will not only be satisfied by this book, they'll be thrilled."
—Dear Reader, *Square Books Newsletter*

PUBLISHED BY W.W. NORTON

AN OLD TESTAMENT

Earl Shorris

IN 1981, I put on my yarmulke and went off to the political wars. They are over now, the *casus belli* is merely history: The left hand can no longer distinguish itself from the right. I do not know who won. It was not me.

Some say it was all because of Stalin and the Moscow trials. Or the ax they sank into the skull of Frida Kahlo's sometime lover, Leon Trotsky. Or the non-aggression pact. Something brought those Jewish intellectuals across the aisle. I've also heard that it was the Sixties, but it couldn't have been the Sixties; I lived in San Francisco then, where I saw that wearing flowers in one's hair was just another bourgeois way to be. To tell the truth, it was Stalin in the early cases, but it was also the discovery by some Jews that, in America, they were white, and therefore finally safe from the racial wars of an immoral world.

This so astonished one fellow from Brooklyn that he soon abandoned his liberal star-gazing and intellectual social climbing and became overnight a racist, homophobe, and public enemy of mercy. With the stout support of his wife, the Brooklyn boy became an evangelist for a new philosophy that he billed as a reinterpretation of the Jewish ethos. Not Jews for Jesus; Jesus had nothing to do with it. The man from Brooklyn and his allies decided that the Jewish way was to put one's own interests first and, yes, even foremost. It was Jews for Reagan, the man who had won more Jewish votes than any Republican candidate in history.

What was a Jewish writer to do, especially one who knew that the corners of the field were to be given to the poor and had read enough Rashi to know that there was also a left hand of God?

I began writing a book about neo-conservative Jews. My first idea for a title had religious overtones: The Apostates. But even as a working title it seemed to drive the book in the wrong direction, toward metaphysics rather than ethics. Then, while looking for something else on my bookshelf (Gogol? Gorky? Goethe?), I came across a book by Mike Gold published in the Thirties. His *Jews Without Money* suggested that I should call my book *Jews Without Mercy* and that it should have a short subtitle, *A Lament*.

It was the first of many errors and miscalculations. I should have stayed with apostasy, if I wanted to avoid a war.

But war is exactly what I wanted. Pod–horetz, Kristol, Hook, Decter, Glazer and

Earl Shorris recently received the National Humanities Medal from the president of the United States. Norman Podhoretz did not.

Co. had been able to move from mercy to justice—the left hand to the right hand of God, according to Rashi—with very little resistance from Jewish liberals. Or anyone else. Silence, I thought, was a danger to democracy as well as ethics, a greater danger than the politics of self-interest and its attendant duplicities (one of the noisiest promoters of self-interest was a magazine called *The Public Interest*). Worse, Glazer's attacks on affirmative action, Podhoretz's transmogrification of a failure of virtú—his "Negro Problem"—into "Ours," Decter's wildly homophobic pronouncements, and Kristol's encomia for the selfish—all, strangely enough, from what they insisted was the Jewish viewpoint—angered and shamed me. Instead of "a light to nations," they were making us into a shadow.

Loretta Barrett, an editor at Anchor Press—the "egghead division of Doubleday"—published the book with expectations of controversy, although not of sales. She went at the publishing of my little gadfly as other people go about guaranteed bestsellers. Galleys went out, advertising was prepared. A quote from Jacobo Timerman, who was then in the news, found its way onto the front of the jacket. *The Nation* published an excerpt. I did not expect an argument against neoconservatism to stir up much controversy with its readers, but the audience was admirable, and I was glad to be there.

At the end of March, two months before publication, the *Boston Globe* did a half-page piece in the Sunday paper featuring large photographs of Daniel Bell, Irving Kristol, Norman Podhoretz, Nathan Glazer and Sidney Hook. Kristol had no comment, Glazer said he hadn't seen the book, but three of the gentlemen did have comments: Podhoretz called the book "garbage." Bell said he found "even the title offensive." And Hook said that the author was "a Jew without scruples." Decter, who was not pictured, called the book "unspeakably ignorant."

Robert Levey's *Globe* story was fair, intelligent, and cleanly written. The neoconservatives responded to the book with invective, nothing more. I knew they would do better later, but for the moment the book seemed to be carrying out its intended function. On publication day two extraordinary things happened: A favorable review by Christopher Lehmann-Haupt appeared in the *New York Times* and I received a telephone call at seven-thirty that morning from an executive on the editorial side of the paper who described the review as "an act of moral courage."

The notion of a book review as an act of moral courage seemed to me absurd. The review hadn't been that good, and I hoped the book was not that bad. But the thought of book reviewing as a moral act set my soul to dancing.

It was the last dance. A silence unlike any I had ever known began. The *New York Times* Sunday books section, which has reviewed every book I have written, with the exception of a first novel long ago, was silent. When someone at the paper brought it up to the editor of the Sunday *Book Review*, he reportedly snapped, "Who wants to know?"

The neoconservative magazines—*Commentary, The Public Interest*—and the more or less Jewish intellectual magazines, with the exception of the *New Leader*, were utterly silent. Loretta Barrett ran an ad in the *New York Times*, with one side devoted to positive comments from Timerman, Victor Navasky, Justin Kaplan, and the Lehmann-Haupt review, as best I can remember, and the other side repeating the invective from the *Globe* story.

Curiously enough, David Brudnoy, a conservative who hosted a Boston radio program, invited me up there one night to talk about the book. My wife and I drove up during a terrible rainstorm. Brudnoy was polite; he had read the book, but it was the day the Israelis chose to bomb Lebanon, and that was the story. Between network reports of the bombing we spoke of death and politics.

Not long afterward, a young editor at *Harper's* told of attending a meeting of the Committee for the Free World, which he said was run by Midge Decter and included Eugene Ionesco and Saul Bellow among its members. One of the subjects of the meeting, according to the young editor, was the book I had written. How to respond to it was the question. The final decision was "to kill it with silence."

The meeting had taken place shortly after the publication of the *Globe* article and before the daily *Times* review. If the members of The Committee for the Free World had indeed used their considerable influence to stifle another

≈ ≈ ≈

SOME DAYS IN THE CITY

Some days, the sky descends to the level of mid-thigh water
the clock-hands come loose, and language is a skiff
over land through the rhythm of your breathing, girl
then I can hear the pink oriole, the body is a metronome
of blood and syllables beating placentas of speech
and news tingles like a caress of words still to be spoken:

umbrellas, bracelets, sleepers in doorways, police and victim—

I wind these objects to strike my human self dead
so as to taste the massy hive, the bloom and sounds
following my spending to gather up the pennies, kisses
meant for you, lost in transit, I follow my own kisses
to rooms in European cities, to the bottom of a shot glass

like a piece of economy flung about the streets
I spit pronouns, you fall from my lips, bewildered
I fall to the tracks, a suicide, a trembling drunk at Du Pont
and this day is a book left ajar, next to the rain.

—Mark McMorris

point of view, their effectiveness was astonishing. Suddenly, the world seemed to have become mute.

Eventually the silence itself became a point of interest to people other than the author, and a few people tried to spark a public discussion. Art D'Lugoff, who owned the Village Gate nightclub, tried to arrange a debate there between liberal/left Jews and neoconservative Jews. Alan Wolfe and I agreed to speak for the liberal/left, but no matter how hard he tried or who he telephoned, none of the neoconservatives who appeared in the book, even in passing, were willing to debate.

Finally, a lesser known woman and Joshua Muravchik, a fellow so young he apparently had not been apprised of the silence decree, agreed to debate. Muravchik was a pleasant enough person, and though it was not an easy night for him, he remained gracious to the end.

Not long afterward, the American Jewish Committee held a board meeting in New York. A member of the board telephoned Loretta Barrett at her office at Anchor Press. She reported the following conversation:

"I am a member of the AJC, here for the meeting, and I would like to put copies of Shorris's book in the hands of the board members."

"Wonderful!" Barrett said. "How many do you need? I'll send them by messenger."

"Forty."

"Where shall I send them?"

"To the hotel."

"All right, and to your attention. Your name?"

"I can't tell you my name. If anyone found out ..."

And that was the end of it. There were no nasty letters, no responses, nothing. The question of whether it was a passion for mercy or for self-interest that had enabled a tiny minority to survive slavery, expulsions, the Inquisition, pogroms, and the ultimate barbarity of Hitler's attempt at genocide was never debated. I pined mightily for the moral exhilaration of dialogue and I mourned the loss of the gorgeous curiosity of a great tradition.

It broke my heart. In my mid-forties I lay in the cardiac care unit in that common debate with death. The thought of Lebanon, the pull of mercy, and a little oxygen conspired to keep me alive.

Upon recovering, I sat on an empty beach and dreamed. Metaphors came to visit there. They made a schedule of work.

Then to put the seal to summer, a friend phoned from New York with news.

"Your book has been reviewed by the *American Spectator*," he said.

"Yes," I said, wondering what gentile conservatives thought about mercy.

"They called you a swine."

✿ ✿ ✿

From Shorris's Jeremiad

THE NEOCONSERVATIVES have forgotten who they are. They have fame, they are close to power as advisers to powerful men, and they remind their audiences that Jews are rich. They do not seem to recall that Jews are few. All of them are teachers or writers, men and women who are comfortable with adulation, at ease with the power of teachers over their students and of editors over writers. Men come in limousines and private planes to seek their wisdom.

Jeremiah described the difference between their position and that of Jewish ethics: "Thus saith the Lord: Let not the wise man glory in his wisdom, neither let the mighty man glory in his might, let not the rich man glory in his riches; but let him that glorieth glory in this, that he understandeth, and knoweth Me, that I am the Lord who exercise mercy, justice, and righteousness, in the earth." (Jer. 9:23)

The ethics of Jeremiah were not born in an ivory tower. If any man knew the ways of the world and the abuses of power, it was Jeremiah. The life of a prophet was a perilous one: If he delivered bad news and it came true, he suffered along with the rest of the people; if he delivered bad news and it did not come true, he might be killed or exiled as a false prophet. Jeremiah's father was sent into exile by King Solomon; the prophet learned early on what a man might endure if he disagreed with the powerful. Jeremiah himself lived through Israel's defeats by the Babylonians and Assyrians. He died in exile in Egypt. He was tried for treason. He endured beatings, curses, prison. His works were shredded and burned. He was thrown into a well and left to die. Treachery, defeat, destruction, murder, corruption, and oppression were all well known to him. Yet he urged Jews to seek the ethical life.

One does not expect a movement of editors and teachers to have either the poetry or the vision or even the worldliness of Jeremiah, nor does one expect such a movement to have the temerity to preach loudly against the ethics that have sustained a people for more than three thousand years.

The neoconservatives might argue that they have a different message precisely because they have not suffered in their own lives. They are the Jews who attended secular universities, gaining prestige and financial security. They are the Jews who send their children to secular universities

and see them move into greater spheres of prosperity and security. They have come through the Judaism of Michael Gold and Henry Roth and Philip Roth. They have come through the Judaism of Abraham Cahan and Clara Lemlich and the ILGWU and Irving Howe. They have come through the Ku Klux Klan and Gerald L. K. Smith and restrictions and quotas. They have come through sweatshops and tenements and the Depression and Brooklyn and the Bronx. They have made it. Jews worked in tanneries and collected dog dung and lived in ghettos, but that was a long time ago. This is America and these are good times for Jews in America.

THE LEADERS of the neoconservative movement do not want to appear in the world as foolish old Jews of the ghetto, crying out for social justice for all, social justice so pervasive that it includes the Jew. Nor do they believe mercy and social justice must be brought about through the law of the land. They are for the strong. They are for the efficiency of the market in all things, for they identify with the strong. Shame for them is to be a poor and humble people and to behave accordingly.

At the heart of their choice, they say, is an abiding belief in the market efficiencies of capitalism. They have wholeheartedly embraced the theory of the invisible hand. It is an interesting theory and very much to the benefit of some, but it is not a theory that can be made compatible with Judaism. The invisible hand devolves from the antinomian ideas of Saul of Tarsus; Jewish ethics devolve from the visible hand of the Law.

THE EYES OF SPIRO ARE UPON YOU
The Myth of the Liberal Media

Chris Lehmann

You fellows got a great ballgame going. As soon as you're through… we're going to do a story on all of you.

—*Former Attorney General John Mitchell to Carl Bernstein, 1972*

AMERICANS ENJOY precious little in the way of cultural consensus, in our feverishly fragmented, post-everything new millennium. But we do know one thing: The media are not to be trusted. The press is like a plague of locusts upon the republic: elitist, biased, and forever ideological.

This axiom of public life commands universal assent, from virtually every point along the political spectrum. Its dominant variant comes from the American right and is, by now, wearily familiar. The lords of the press, we are told, use the machinery of mass persuasion to mint a steady stream of agitprop briefs for the liberal order. So widespread has this plaint become that, in a paradox worthy of a Howard Beale, vilifying the elite liberal media has become the fastest path to elite media success. Even though Bill O'Reilly of Fox News, for example, has written the best-selling political book of the year 2000, commands a market share

in the cable talk world rivalled only by Larry King, and recently signed a six-year contract for $24 million, he still claims that he devotes himself to "things not presented in the elite media." For good measure O'Reilly also likes to point out that he drives "a 1994 automobile" every day to work. (Forced to concede that the vehicle in question was a Lexus, he protested, "But you know it's a 1994—it's got some dings in it.")

O'Reilly is wrong about many things, but he is right to suppose that his credentials as an opponent of all things elite can be established by referring to his personal bearing and taste preferences. It's not, after all, that O'Reilly or anyone else accuses the "liberal media" of ramming home some identifiable tradition or system of thought. That is never the charge. No, the malevolent liberalism that is so frequently found to taint the operations of the press always turns out to be a matter of "bias," of the character and image of the news' deliverers. The very terminology of the indictment is revealingly personal and pathological in its overtones: Before the late Sixties "bias" was largely a clinical term from the social sciences, used to describe the irrational attitudes held by bigots, discriminators, and the generally backward. Bias was an involuntary or irrational impulse, to be brought to light and then duly diagnosed, treated, and cured.

In the view of the right, liberalism was the real bias that infected our culture. And the underlying disorder of which liberalism was a symptom was that most loathsome of social dysfunctions, class snobbery. Liberals were liberal because they were self-important know-it-alls, insulated in their Eastern seaboard from the real-world consequences of their bad ideas—and for that matter, from the real world generally. They adored militant blacks and protesters, but wouldn't let them near their fine homes (or their privileged daughters). They wanted to desegregate the schools, so long as they could raise their own kids in lavishly funded lily-white suburban districts. The only workers they encountered were in Peter, Paul, and Mary's rendition of "Joe Hill."

This key plank of the bias complaint proved to be its greatest political legacy: a readily deployed, infinitely adaptable rhetoric of pseudo-populism. Although the "media elite" in question—reporters, news readers, editors—weren't owners or plutocrats in the way that traditional populist villains were, the idea that the anchorman's unflappability or the journalist's questioning were merely markers of "snobbery," of a detestable sense of superiority, caught on immediately and has never left us.

Indeed, the basic terms of the bias myth have swollen to engulf the entire nation. In the aftermath of the recent contest to elect the nation's new Fundraiser-in-Chief, it dawned simulta-neously on nearly every pundit in the land that there were, in fact, "two Americas": one based in the South and West—the mythic homeland of the common man—that turned out in droves for the privileged scion of a Republican political dynasty; and one sequestered in the nation's coasts and big cities—those dens of cosmopolitanism and foreign influence—that preferred the privileged scion of a Democratic political dynasty. But while the pundit set busily contemplated this graphic reminder of the villainy of the liberal elite, what may have been the most consequential instance of media distortion in our history went largely unremarked. In the twilight hours of the second Wednesday in November, a producer for Fox News called the state of Florida, and with it the presidency, for the Republican nominee (who also happened to be his cousin) without any empirical basis for doing so, thus setting in motion the irresistible narrative of a state rightfully won by Republicans, and then targeted for cunning post facto thievery by power-mad liberal elitists—and (worse!) their retinue of attorneys.

Not even the most significant facts, in other words, are capable of derailing the liberal bias myth. In view of this samurai-like devotion to the bias critique in all its solemn, pointless varieties, it's high time to furnish some historical grounding to the whole gaseous phenomenon. The bias complaint is, after all, but a recent offspring of our political scene. Over the course of most of its commercialized, modern career, the press was quite straightforwardly taken to be an instrument of reactionary vanity—owned, operated, and strategically leased by the

WHAT THE MEDIA AREN'T TELLING YOU

About Dubya's Cabinet. In contrast to the kid-gloves treatment given by most of the mainstream media, *The Nation* reached some blunt conclusions in a series of informed investigations of George W. Bush's Cabinet appointees. Our take on the new Attorney General: "John Ashcroft is not just a conservative. He stands at the place where the Christian fanatics, antichoicers, militiamen, gun nuts and white supremacists come together."

About the Secret History of Lead. In an exhaustive special report, *The Nation* showed how General Motors, Standard Oil and Du Pont colluded to make and market gasoline containing lead—a deadly poison—although there were safe alternatives. Abetted by the US government, they suppressed scientific evidence that lead kills. Still sold in countries all over the world, leaded gasoline continues to poison the planet.

About Abortion Rights. As columnist Katha Pollitt noted, the new threats to reproductive rights are frequently of the less-publicized variety, like localized legal attacks against abortion providers—an example being the recent trumped-up charges of extortion leveled against a Florida doctor. The message: "If the arsonists don't get you, litigation may."

is only in The Nation.

About the Battle in Seattle. "Seattle was indeed a milestone of a new kind of politics. Labor shed its nationalism for a new rhetoric of internationalism and solidarity. Progressives replaced their apologetic demeanor of the past twenty years with confidence, style and wit."

About Nuclear Weapons. As our examination of the fine print hidden within our new President's emerging nuclear doctrine showed, "George W. Bush is taking advice from a group of unreformed initiates in the nuclear priesthood who are desperately seeking ways to relegitimize nuclear weapons."

About the FBI. An intensive investigation for *The Nation* turned up everything from slovenly casework to massively skewed priorities. Example: Number of convictions for health and safety violations against employees in a single year: one. Number of telephone taps: 1.3 million.

Want to know more? More than you'll ever learn from the corporate-owned major media? Covering everything from Washington and Wall Street to the latest books, films, culture and art? Subscribe to America's oldest, nosiest, most independent weekly journal of fact and opinion.

titans of industry and lovingly molded into whatever image of the country's body politic they happened to prefer. Think of the storied press lords of prewar vintage—the good and great Messrs. Chandler, Hearst, or McCormick, whose papers bestraddled the nation's great metropolises through the first half of the twentieth century—and you have summoned the shades of some of the nation's most bloodthirsty, most unapologetic paleo-cons. And even at the height of the Republican outrage over liberal bias, the nation's newspapers endorsed Richard Nixon over George McGovern by a ratio of 753 to fifty-six.

But that sort of thing has never mattered much in the fury-filled world of the backlash. The emergence of the liberal bias critique was, indeed, a sort of willed act of secession on the part of the right— the first flourish of what would be a thirty-year cultural counterrevolution. And so powerful did the bias indictment prove to be that during the Seventies (and Eighties, and Nineties, and probably the Oughts too) it got worked up into an all-purpose assault on every leading institution of cultural authority—the university, the judiciary, Hollywood, the literary establishment—all of them now dismissed with the blanket epithet of "the New Class."

From Idiot Box to Ideology Box

IN ITS BEGINNINGS, the bias complaint was, as befits the Age of McLuhan, a question of medium, not message. Horrified by the unruly tumult of Sixties antiwar and civil rights protests, conservatives saw a decade's worth of happy Cold War consensus slipping away, and concluded that the culprit was… *television.*

The argument is almost plausible on paper. A new medium matures into a mass information organ—indeed, the leading source of news, by the time of the Nixon years. It traffics, both for formal reasons of genre and commercial considerations of audience maintenance, in oversimplification and colorful visual sensation. At the same time, dramatic new forms of social discontent sweep across the land—in particular among the country's privileged young, who have spent enormous quantities of time laying about absorbing vast undifferentiated swaths of the cool blue medium's nightly output.

Ergo, *they must be getting their marching orders from the networks!* It was unthinkable, after all, that the civil rights movement had incubated among black church leaders, union representatives, and crusading attorneys ever since the cruelly broken promises of Reconstruction. And certainly no reputable American leader or opinion maker would have decided on their own to question the principles of Cold War containment then on singularly grim display in Vietnam. Reasoned, historically grounded dissent from consensus Americanism was simply not imaginable.

So all the compass points on the question of the press were demagnetized nearly overnight. Suddenly the stolid array of station managers, big city press lords, and fledgling TV barons who had done so much to foment uncritical Americanism, shore up civic boosterism, and (last but not least) break the back of organizing drives in their own sunny open shops became, via the sort of polemical alchemy that is only possible in America, "the liberal media."

For all practical purposes, the Magna Carta of the liberal media critique is Spiro Agnew's firebreathing November 1969 speech, "The Television News Medium," which he delivered, significantly, in Des Moines, Iowa. Taking as his text a recent TV address on Vietnam strategy by his boss, Richard Nixon, the vice president deplored the "instant analysis and querulous criticism" doled out over the airwaves by "a small band of network commentators and self-appointed analysts, the majority of whom expressed their hostility to what [Nixon] had to say." Warming to his subject, Agnew dubbed the influence wielded by this petulant band of naysayers "a concentration of power over American public opinion unknown in history." These "men can create national issues overnight," Agnew declared, and by supplying a thumbnail profile of this sinister cadre, he left little doubt as to the quality and timbre of the "issues" they were inventing for nightly broadcast. "Of the commentators, most Americans know little other than that they reflect an urbane and assured presence seemingly well-informed on every important matter," Agnew claimed, his

The Big Lullaby

of The ex-Veep

words dripping with populist contempt. "We do know that to a man these commentators live and work in the geographical and intellectual confines of Washington, D.C., or New York City, the latter of which James Reston terms the most unrepresentative community on earth."[†]

Representative or no, New York and all of its coded rhetorical baggage—liberal, decadent, educated, elite, and (hardly inconsequential in these matters) Jewish—proved to be just the sort of symbol that the American right needed. If the

---

[†] The invocation of *New York Times* Washington hand James "Scotty" Reston must have given Agnew's audience a moment's pause. Reston was, of course, an avatar of the New York and Washington press establishments, a consummate insider who was once moved to run an article credited, "By Henry Kissinger with James Reston." Reston's political reflexes were far more representative of the Washington–New York axis than any of the hypothetical "band" of network officials that Agnew darkly summons here. But then Agnew's speech was composed by none other than Pat Buchanan, himself a native of Washington and a former editorial writer for the *St. Louis Post-Dispatch*. Just as Agnew's speech bred a whole right-wing theology of "bias," so did it mark the de facto launching of Buchanan's own long-running career as the arch insider masquerading as Middle American outsider.

media were minting student radicals out of the suburbs and lavishing black militants with airtime and book contracts, why, then, the solution was to demonize the media. All of Agnew's most reliable applause lines—"the impudent snobs" and "nattering nabobs of negativity"—were aimed to smear the press as a haughty band of high hats. And they resounded magnificently, much more so than any strategist could have dreamed. After all, the surest path to saturation coverage in the media is to assault the media—as subsequent generations of right-wing media baiters, from Dan Quayle to Newt Gingrich to Dick Armey, have found in the long decades since.

More importantly, the Agnew assault also produced a dramatic new topography of American politics, forever muddling the all-important mythos of social class. According to the bias critique, the blue-collar hardhats and the owning class were part of the same persecuted cultural majority, united by their shared marginalization in the press. In the backlash vision, owner and worker stood together in defense of the besieged values of Americanism; whatever differences they had were dwarfed by the colossal arrogance of the real class enemy, the media.

Agnew took pains to assure his listeners on that day in Des Moines that by attacking the dastardly liberal media he was not advocating censorship. Instead, as he put it, he was simply "asking whether a form of censorship already exists when the news that forty million Americans receive each night is determined by a handful of men responsible only to their corporate employers and is filtered through a handful of commentators who admit to their own set of biases."

Of course, the answer to Agnew's question was "no." Not only was the vice president here confusing censorship—the suppressing of news—with news judgment, with the *reporting* of news (news that's sometimes unwelcome in official quarters), but he was also assuming, as nearly every critic of liberal bias has ever since, that the media are a simple manufactory of political boilerplate. This entailed a great deal of political distortion in its own right, hinging upon a pair of breathtakingly contradictory claims. American citizen-viewers were, on the one hand, taken to be as suggestible as obedient puppies, schooled by the sheer repetitive force of soothing liberal voices into questioning the day's ration of napalm raining over the Vietnamese countryside. On the other hand, however, Agnew's populist reform prescription held that networks should rightfully be reflecting the magisterial will and tastes of the common man, held but moments ago to be helplessly transfixed by daily doses of liberal sophistication.

But all squares are circled under the inviting master narrative of bias: Broadcasting is censorship; viewers are both dupes of the elites and omnicompetent citizens; the executive branch of the world's most powerful government is oppressed by a small band of fast-talking New Yorkers. It is all, you see, a matter of ideology. And ideology is an agent capable of producing every imaginable social distortion. Throughout his indictment, Agnew supposes that the stealth bacillus of ideology travels untainted and unfiltered through each layer of the bureaucracy hulking behind every network news logo. Of necessity, news copy must bear the fatal imprint of the political proclivities of whatever decision-maker finally looses it into the broadcast booth.

That this is not an accurate depiction of how network news broadcasts are conceived and redacted is to understate things, well, exponentially. Just consider, for example, the world of presumption squeezed into Agnew's abbreviated disclaiming clause, "responsible only to their corporate employers." Those employers were not merely old Cold War propaganda hands such as CBS's William Paley, but more generally—and far more depressingly—earnest gray men of the company, conditioned to regard ideas and opinions of any ideological or, indeed, merely controversial pedigree as nothing short of business-destroying sedition. This is not to say they were engines of right-wing ideology, either—just that they were, and for the most part, continue to be stunningly idea-resistant. As Richard S. Salant, president of CBS News, famously told *TV Guide* in the late Sixties, "Our reporters do not cover stories from *their* point of view. They are presenting them from *nobody's* point of view."

No conspiracy of sinister cosmopolitans is required to explain this state of affairs. Rather, the enterprising media critic only needs to reference the blinding truth that any casual viewer of TV instantly grasps in a good ten minutes of

∾ ∾ ∾

AUTOGRAPHEME

A thought on the lip of little sand island, an easy messenger who forgot where to go. I came to laugh in a dirty garden, a thwarted pauselessness considering pearls. I was fluent in salamander. Everything wrote itself onto skin with a tangled blowing. Identity washed its trousers just off-shore. An opal eye looking down on an errant package. A sky wrung of tint. What is the meaning of this minor error? The reflecting pool no one could read. A beach fire snagged me with its bright emergent eye. I was buttoned to Africa. My colony sought revolt in every yard. The present was a relic of a past I was older than. Taking its language, I became an abridgment of whatever I contained, a social imperative of silky fears. I wanted air. I wanted the balloon. Darkness flaked down like bottle glass invented by a poor oily sea. A house made of soup. The others formed an invisible order felt in every part. The male of the species was louder than the female. Females cowered, they made the mush, a sound of off-stage sweeping. Boys played a game of torture and sleepy forgiveness while girls read their books on the rocks, containers of a solar plot. Little bird, fox on a string. A caravan of foreign number, staging death. So? A smudge against the smallest dress, buried creature. Of sly erasures in the storied night, long *e* cricketing awake, asleep.

— Elizabeth Willis

viewing time: All network content is designed to serve as a lubricant for the
streamlined transmission of advertising.
The last thing advertisers want are audiences absorbing and pondering system-
atic political analysis—which is why, in
the network bazaar of ad buys, the long-
est advertising dollars go either to the
most lurid or most vacuous fare. Network
news broadcasts function primarily as audience placeholders, as gateways to the
main programming events in primetime,
where the biggest ad buys reign. As such,
they strive not to emphasize or screen out
facts according to some neo-aristocratic
imperative, but just the opposite: to
achieve a programming tone of deathly
noncommitment, a sustained, numbing
impression of authorial absence.

Agnew, however, saw a political opportunity amid all the strategic no-speak of
the network news. "As with other American institutions, perhaps it is time that the
networks were made more responsive to
the people they serve," Agnew announced,
and went on to note that the people's own
humble servants—the leaders perched at
the executive branch's very pinnacle—
now served at the whim of the network
commissariat: "Every elected leader in
the United States depends on the media.
Whether what I've said to you tonight
will be heard and seen at all by the nation is not my decision, it's not your decision, it's their decision."

With this felicitous bait and switch,
political reasoning had gone through the

looking glass—and not simply because
Agnew's speech got lavish coverage the
next day in both the print and broadcast
media. Cloaked in the sonorous language
of objectivity, fairness, and neutrality,
what Agnew delivered was a call for *representation:* a demand that the media supply a map of right-wing opinion corre-
sponding precisely to the broad ideological profile of the national electorate.[†]

As Agnew successfully framed the question, what was important about the media
wasn't such tedious, empirical matters
as affiliate licensing, cable regulation,
and local broadcast fiefdoms; no, it was
all about cultural *attitudes*, about the
haughty bearing and perversely "urbane"
views of a "small band of men" ensconced
at strategic points along the country's
Eastern seaboard.

Revolt of the Burghers

THE LIBERAL bias plaint may be largely
imaginary, but the ability of journalists to disrupt or discredit certain initiatives of the executive branch has always
been real. For the paranoid Richard
Nixon himself, the conflict had a personal
edge as well. Long willing to remind any
and all listeners of his bitter resentment
at being "kicked around" by the American
press, he took the first chance he could to
declare war. When the general subject of
the press came up, Nixon was once able
to announce to his cabinet, straightfaced,
that "We've got a counter-government

[†] A subordinate irony of the long-running rightist uproar over liberal media bias is that it has accompanied thirty years of unambiguous electoral triumphs for the right. This suggests, among other things,
that if liberals have in fact been running amok in the network sanctums, it would be in the right's political interest just to let them be.

here and we've got to fight it." Yet Nixon faced a delicate logistical problem as he went into battle against the media. There was little hope of demonizing an institution that was draped in the sacrosanct protections of the First Amendment—and that, as a practical matter, was fully capable of conducting its own greatly public counterattacks.

So Nixon took up the fight with the trademark divide-and-conquer strategy of the backlash. His targets were the network execs so reviled by Agnew, and his allies would be the rock-ribbed Republicans who owned most TV and radio franchises. By setting the interests of one against those of the other, Nixon could both silence troublemakers and enrich his supporters. In his first term in office Nixon set up an "Office of Telecommunications Policy"—a cabinet-level outfit that sprang from no clear White House organizational or policy mandate. The agency's chairman, Clay T. Whitehead, proceeded to translate Agnew's outbursts into a series of carefully crafted policy grenades, which he lobbed over the heads of the local franchise owners and into the jittery boardrooms of the "small band" of network executives. Whitehead laid much of the groundwork for the cost-cutting moguls' playground we now call the telecommunications industry. According to the 1971–1972 *Alfred I. DuPont-Columbia University Survey of Broadcast Journalism*, Whitehead "called for all the things the broadcasters had been clamoring for

over the years and a few they wouldn't have dared mention: the deregulation of radio, the scuttling of the Fairness Doctrine, getting the government out of programming by revising the license-renewal process, and by implication the rewriting of the Communications Act of 1934."

Even though the last of these would not be enacted until the Clinton administration and the Telecommunications Act of 1996, the foundations of today's digitally driven media cartel were being built in those heady early days of the backlash.

All this hectic deregulation and deal-brokering was sold to the public not as a way to build more monopolies and media billionaires, but instead to liberate broadcast journalism—and the impressionable public—from its unmanly thrall to elite liberal groupthink. As Whitehead sternly chided the annual meeting of the press fraternity Sigma Delta Chi in 1972, "The First Amendment's guarantee of a free press was not supposed to create a privileged class of men called journalists, who are immune to criticism by government or restraint by publishers and editors." No, this was a class war in which the interests of the common people were to be protected by corporate management. For, as Whitehead continued, "Who else but management... can assure that the audience is being served by journalists devoted to the highest professional standards? Who else but management can or should correct so-called professionals who confuse sensationalism with sense and who dispense elitist gossip in the guise of news analysis?"

But who, exactly, was this "management"? Despite Whitehead's ringing evocation of the solid corporate citizen,

"management" remains the missing link in the endless culture wars over media bias. It was, however, quite easy for his audience to grasp the simple point Whitehead was making: The "management" Whitehead was invoking was perched atop the hundreds of local TV affiliates that bestride our great nation. These mid-market executives were—and for the most part, still are—the runty, right-wing tails that wag the supposedly all-powerful network dogs; they control the places that register the first, and certainly the most influential, uproars over "controversial" TV fare, be it an unseemly or unpatriotic investigative piece, a perceived slight to believers, or a lesbian kiss.

Few of the professional critics of the liberal media take note of the network affiliates. This is because doing so would be pretty much fatal to the sport of deriding the remote, out-of-touch cultural elites who are thought to manipulate the levers of network transmission. In his 1973 book, News From Nowhere—still by far the most rigorously researched and documented study of the production, distribution, and strategic vetting of network news—Edward Epstein pointed out that the real power in broadcasting is held by the networks' local affiliates. Not only did they possess legal authority over broadcast content, but they were also the building blocks by which networks sold national audiences to national advertisers, generating those corporate goods that were such supposed anathema to liberals—profits and operating revenues. And who, exactly, ran these affiliate operations? As one network vice president confided to Epstein: "Affiliates tend to be owned by people in another business—

newspapers, automobile dealers, Coke distributors—and run by salesmen and former announcers. Their politics are Republican, their ideals are pragmatic and their preoccupation with return on invested capital and the safety of their license to broadcast is total."

As a result, any network-produced news feature that strayed too far into unseemly political controversy—most notoriously the 1971 CBS documentary on Vietnam PR initiatives, "The Selling of the Pentagon"—would send affiliate owners rising up to denounce it, and (more importantly) refusing to air it, producing an uncomfortable reminder to already hard-pressed network news divisions of how costly controversy can be. Not to mention how politicized: During a congressional inquiry into that documentary's production, CBS president Frank Stanton actually went to jail for denying Congress access to footage edited out of the broadcast. (Nor was this the most dramatic affiliate-inspired foray into the nation's politics: An ambitious manager of the Raleigh, North Carolina, ABC affiliate named Jesse Helms made liberal bias a central plank of his maiden Senate run in 1972, demanding that network news divisions be dismantled outright, and the airtime for national news relegated entirely to local markets.)

None of this affiliate/network animus was lost on the policy-making arm of the Nixon White House. Indeed, followers of the administration's high-profile war with the media must have been astonished by the number of occasions the White House took to romance local broadcasters. In June 1972, Nixon hosted thirty local station owners and executives at a White

New dimensions of dementia

House dinner at which he assured his guests that he would stabilize the process of license renewal and suppress a troublesome FTC proposal to force fraudulent advertisers to run "counter-advertisements" confessing their wrongdoing. The following week, 110 local on-air news personalities turned out for a White House briefing and reception. All this activity bore out the shrewd 1971 appraisal of the unnamed observer who said, after the administration called for the repeal of the Fairness Doctrine and the overhaul of the 1934 Telecommunications Act, "If I were the Republican National Committee, I'd set up about fifty dummy committees to handle the broadcaster contributions that are going to be coming in."

Thus we propose, as a general axiom of the American culture wars: Any time officialdom begins laying into remote and manipulative elites, see if the burghers start to nod their assent.

THE RIGHT'S WAR on the media paid off handsomely. For conservative politicians, it yielded a potent variant of populism they could call their own. For the affiliate owners, prosperity came with the waves of deregulation that followed in the wake of the new populists' electoral victories. The campaign donations rolled in—not just to Nixon, but to his market-happy successors Reagan and Bush, and in good time, the broadcasting donor class got everything it paid for. First came children's television, which was transformed under Reagan FCC chair Mark ("Television is just a toaster with pictures") Fowler into a long parade of badly animated advertorial features, produced by cheap overseas syndicates. Then came the local news revolution, loosening the FCC's already rudimentary fairness and standards-and-practices regimes and bringing forth the rich ferment of depoliticized ghoulishness and happy talk that is today duplicated with eerie sameness in every major market.

In addition, the cable explosion produced robust new revenue streams for local owners—and eroded network viewership to the point that the Big Three no longer command the attention of a majority of the country's viewing households, a development that renders the media bias complaint even more objectively idle than it was thirty years ago. The still cheaper and far more ideological medium of talk radio, meanwhile, is experiencing explosive market growth. And with deregulation, cable and radio have been bundled together into enormous audience-delivery systems for advertisers—and for overtly ideological broadcasting moguls of the right such as Rupert Murdoch. (Indeed, the thought of any of today's network or cable presidents landing in the hoosegow for shielding their news operations from hostile government

scrutiny, as CBS's Stanton did in 1971, can call forth nothing but a torrent of bitter guffaws.)

As a result of these dramatic market shifts, it is quite impossible to name more than a handful of avowedly liberal commentators on the burgeoning broadcast empires of cable and talk radio combined. On the right? Let's see... Tony Snow, Brit Hume, Laura Ingraham, Bill O'Reilly, John McLaughlin, Mary Matalin, Sean Hannity, and Alan Combs. And that's just cable; talk radio has coughed forth such lovely specimens of temperate debate as Das Limbaugh, Dr. Laura, Gordon Liddy, Larry Elder, Bob Grant, Ollie North, Don Imus, and Neal Boortz. Nor does any of this take into account the obscenely lavish spectrum giveaway known as the Telecommunications Act of 1996, which is sure to launch another tidal wave of low-cost conservative commentary as it, too, efficiently graduates a new class of broadcast burghers into New Economy moguldom—but that is a tangled, grimly instructive policy tale for another occasion.

The Culture Snub

ALL THESE quantum rightward realignments of the media market have taken place as the right has steadily insisted, in shriller and shriller tones, that the media is getting worse and worse. In the first flush of the Reagan era, the networks would be reviled as fonts of "secularism" and doyennes of decadence by newly ascendant prophets of the right (many of them, such as Brothers Falwell and Robertson, commanding sprawling regional media empires of their own).

Neoconservatives would deride the networks for downplaying the Soviet threat, indulging the sexual and feminist revolutions, and mollycoddling criminals in news broadcasts. And come the Nineties, the right would appropriate the elastic lefty epithet of "political correctness," and the sham war against the liberal media elite would start all over again.

This seems, at first, a paradox: The more the right controls the economic structure of the media, the more freely do its leaders bandy the fiction of their cultural persecution. But such is the twisted logic of culture warfare. By honing in on programming content and sidestepping the media industry's economic structure, conservatives are able to endlessly restage all the classic battles of the founding chapter in our culture wars, in the manner of a power-mad chapter of the Society for Creative Anachronism. Those endlessly debatable matters of attitude, language pitch, and representation, they have found, always trump mundane questions such as ownership and allocation of corporate resources.

Not that conservatives shun the quantitative approach altogether. On the contrary, over the years they have transformed bias spotting from a matter of spare-time grumbling into a curiously positivist undertaking, a profession for scholars and think tanks. Strictly speaking, this grant-sopping enterprise dates back to the 1971 publication of the frenetic bias classic *The News Twisters*, by former *TV Guide* editor Edith Efron. It was the tireless Efron's conviction that the dread operation of liberal insinuation was performed not by formal content, editorial decision, or even production values. In-

stead, she sought to document bias much as Secretary of Defense Robert McNamara sought to document victory in Vietnam: By ruthlessly toting up the day's margin of advantage by each opposing side. But whereas McNamara counted body bags, Efron counted individual *words*, words that, in her clumsily conceived "content analysis," bore meanings that threatened to upend the very foundations of the American republic. To encounter one of Efron's copiously annotated bar graphs contrasting the number of words broadcast "for" and "against" some hot-button issue or constituency—"black militants," "the Vietcong," and "violent protesters" on the one hand; the quietly noble "white middle class" on the other—is to behold a peculiar form of right-wing dadaism, an

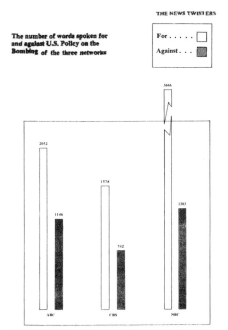

THE NEWS TWISTERS

The number of words spoken for and against U.S. Policy on the Bombing of the three networks

For . . . . . ☐
Against . . . ■

Opinion of "White Middle Class" includes opinion of "white America," "the white American majority," "white racist America," "the white middle-class majority," etc.

unwittingly arch commentary on the bi-
polar wasteland that we now accept as
political reality.

It's tempting to dismiss Efron's divina-
tions of universal liberal bias as the delusions of a lone crank with a foundation
grant. But from her kernel of empirical
affront—the timeless plaint that the networks stubbornly *refused to see things like
she did*—sprang the mighty oak, and
countless swarthy branches, of conservative media demonology. Like the ghost of
Tom Joad, this weird epistemology of
media persecution has surfaced everywhere over the last thirty years that
neoconservatives, New Rightists, Moral
Majoritarians, Reaganites, Dittoheads,
and Gingrich devotees have sought out a
public hearing.

Reed Irvine's Accuracy in Media, founded in 1969, continues to promulgate elabo-
rate conspiracy theories on such pet
right-wing hobby horses as Vincent
Foster's death and the Elián Gonzales
raid. Meanwhile, L. Brent Bozell superin-
tends the Media Research Center, which
carries on over all manner of broadcasting
slaps at the good and the faithful, tirelessly
tabulating such outrages as the moment
when "actress Christine Lahti heralded on
HBO how [sic] Hillary has 'a huge amount
of compassion for people' "; the various
reasons to believe that CNN's Christiane
Amanpour may be soft on Cuba; and—I
hope you're sitting down—an episode in
which a CNN commentator expressed actual "sarcasm on anti-communism."

The MRC has a book-publishing division as well, which, alongside a parade of
paranoid accounts of Clinton's Rasputin-
like hold on the media, has issued one of
the most inadvertently entertaining dia-

tribes in the history of media criticism:
*Out of Focus: Network Television and the
American Economy,* by Burton Yale Pines.
The book chronicles a grim period in
1992, when Pines and an MRC research
associate sat down before a pile of video-
taped network and cable broadcasts and
took diligent stock of the networks' failure to broadcast flat-out laissez-faire propaganda as news. Like most right-wing
media critics, Pines detects a torrent of
covert anti-market messages smuggled
into network entertainment programming. The affronts are tabulated with
ruthless, Efronesque efficiency: "In total,
businesspersons accounted for sixty-six
of the 154 criminals, or 43 percent" of the
law-challenged characters appearing in
the sample of TV entertainment Pines so
diligently monitored. Among the cruel
caricatures: "A classic car dealer fronted
for thieves who stole Bonetti's car in the
January 31 episode of CBS's *Tequila and
Bonetti*"; "Minton, a liquor distributor in
the August 8 episode of ABC's *MacGyver,*
was a gun supplier and murderer."

Loosed in the harrowing sanctums of
the entertainment Moloch, Pines evidently couldn't bring himself to admit
that he's uncovered nothing more sensa-
tional than the age-old device of giving
TV villains, you know, day jobs. But
things get stranger still when Pines trains
his unsparing, bias-mad vision on the
nightly news. After reviewing a CNN report on a nationwide high in teen fatali-
ties at fast-food restaurants, for example,
Pines starts in with some actuarial cavil-
ing: "More teens could have been dying in
fast-food restaurants... not because the
jobs were more dangerous than others,
but simply because more teens were

working in fast-food restaurants than anywhere else."

You know how it is: Put enough teenagers anywhere, and it's just a matter of time before they start keeling over. But such sentimental oversights are not the heart of the problem, in Pines's view: Again, the media is reproached not so much for its active distortions, but for its telltale ideological *silence*. Pines scores the downbeat focus on workplace death for its "failure to tell viewers about the extraordinary role played by fast-food chains in preparing huge numbers of inner-city teenagers for the working world. ... Rather than being dead-end, low-skilled employment for these teens, fast-food outlets have become apprenticeship launching pads to better jobs."

Even if this sunny claim were demonstrable, it would have little actual bearing on the question of on-the-job safety—unless Pines were to blithely contend that the 139 teen corpses are a small price to pay for procuring access to these "launch-

ing pads" of young urban entrepreneurship "whatever the dangers of the job." (One could make a similar argument on behalf of the illegal drug trade, after adjusting for higher body counts in tandem with higher net revenues.) And it's hard to avoid noting another painfully obvious irony here: Even as the right hysterically fingers the media as the de facto stage manager of the late-Nineties outbreak of school shootings, it can apparently shrug off three-figure body counts when a poorly regulated market regime is the obvious culprit.

But such brutal empirical concerns have never been the real point of compulsive bias-spotting. The goal is to feed, water, and nurture cultural resentment in every venue where it can conceivably take root. And in so doing the sport of bias-cataloguing has produced a fine historical irony all its own. Pawing through great heaps of masscult for the most outlandish of ideological affronts, the commandants of the Kulturkampf have overlooked the key consideration that ideology has never mattered less than it does in our own market-addled age. In successive, self-destructive feints of cultural warfare, the American right has found itself exactly where it previously scripted the scheming liberals in its pet passion plays: Despising the country's dominant culture, shrilly insisting on the politicization of private life, composing tract after tract teeming with cranky alarmist persecution, setting themselves up as professional know-it-alls. The titles alone betray this sense of pure and utmost exclusion: *The Tempting of America, The Death of Outrage, The Re-Moralization of America, Experiments Against Reality.*

Meanwhile, according to the right's own reckoning, the basic terms by which the old logic of "bias" operated—all-powerful network elites cunningly orchestrating the behavior of the credulous masses—have fatally broken down. By the magic of the market, Americans now enjoy the right to have their intelligence insulted by the cable broadcaster of their choice. And as a New Economy has replaced the old regime that sought to regulate market growth, it has rendered irrelevant the old criteria of balance and fairness even to their one-time enforcers. Joel Klein, the former trustbuster so reviled by libertarians for his dogged pursuit of Microsoft, now labors for the

Bertelsmann culture conglomerate. All of the last five chairmen of the FCC now work, as either CEOs or attorneys, for brave new Net startups. The most recent convert, Reed Hundt, the Clinton appointee who left the commission in 1997, has even composed his own New Economy memoir, *You Say You Want a Revolution.* He also possesses a multimillion-dollar stock options fortune, gathered from various fledgling digital enterprises; in 1999, he brokered a deal in which Paul Allen, Microsoft's cofounder, poured $355 million into Allegiance Telecom, one of the many corporate boards that has bid frantically to include Hundt in its ranks. Hundt's predecessor in the Bush administration, Alfred C. Sikes, is now president of Hearst Interactive Media, with similar portfolio-pleasing experiences. Yesterday's regulators have become tomorrow's populists of the market. The revolt of the burghers is complete; Spiro Agnew, RIP.

~ ~ ~

IF TODAY YOU GET HIS MEMO, HARDEN NOT YOUR HEARTS

God, this organization is perpetually on the road to the future: relocating, reorganizing, revising, restructuring, retooling, reinventing. And all this change results in an endless string of bruises, dislocations, cuts, strains, and breaks. No matter how I do it, and no matter how necessary it is, every change hurts someone. Comfort me, Father, so your healing can flow to those I lead.

Firing people is the worst of all, God. When I have to tell people that they don't fit the needs of the organization or we can't afford them, they feel betrayed. When they joined us, I told them how important they were, and now no matter how I say it, my message makes them feel unimportant—to us or to anyone else. Maybe not even important to you.

Oh, God, heal these wounds.

—From "Loss," in *Leadership Prayers*, by Richard Kriegbaum (Tyndale House,1998)

40 THE BAFFLER

CHICAGO '72

The Panthers, the Trib, and the
Night My Dad's Yacht Got Hit By a Bus

John R. MacArthur

WHEN FUTURE HISTORIANS of twentieth century American politics go looking for a single scene with which to encapsulate the Great Reaction against Sixties radicalism and reform—now mercilessly barreling toward its fourth decade—they might do well to examine the harshly lit and windswept corner of South Michigan Avenue and the Congress Parkway in Chicago as it appeared on the chilly, forbidding night of November 3, 1972. I happened to be there, shivering in line outside the magnificent old Auditorium Theater with a couple of high school classmates and our history teacher, hoping to get into the big Democratic Party rally scheduled for that evening. The atmosphere was one of electric doom: Even the most optimistic among us knew deep down that this only-in-Chicago, machine-orchestrated campaign event signaled the death throes of the party reform movement that had begun in the late Sixties. Fighting in those years against the party oligarchy that had steered the country into the Vietnam War, anti-war leader Allard Lowenstein and

Potence
(XVIᵉ s.).

Senator Eugene McCarthy had, incredibly, driven an incumbent president from office—and for a time it seemed they might overthrow the entire structure presided over by LBJ and Richard J. Daley, the mayor of Chicago.

And even though Senator George McGovern, the Democratic candidate for president, was one of the party's insurgent leaders, everyone could see the end was near. President Richard Nixon was running for re-election on yet another new "peace" plan called "Vietnamization," and McGovern was far behind in the polls. The handwriting was clearly posted on the wall, or, on this evening at least, the wildly flapping sail of a twenty-four-foot yacht implausibly situated on the east side of Michigan Avenue, bow pointing north, perched on a trailer. The boat belonged to my highly eccentric father, Roderick, and the slogan printed in gigantic black letters on the vessel's mainsail, now billowing in and out with the wind, reflected not only the captain's rage at the corrupt American political system but also the dashed cause of peace: It said,

John R. MacArthur, a former reporter for the *Chicago Sun-Times*, is the publisher of *Harper's Magazine* and the author, most recently, of *The Selling of Free Trade: NAFTA, Washington, and the Subversion of American Democracy*.

simply, and absurdly, "Republicans for McGovern."

Standing in line with my classmates, I'd already heard the jokes about the crazy guy with the boat on Michigan, but I knew my father well and accepted the remarks with silent amusement. Whatever people said about him, Dad usually had a clear and sane objective, no matter what he was peddling, and this nutty, yacht-borne slogan seemed just the right rejoinder to John Connally's highly effective "Democrats for Nixon." Until the 1972 campaign, Connally was best known for sharing a bullet with JFK in Dallas, serving three terms as Democratic governor of Texas, and then switching sides to become Nixon's secretary of the treasury. More importantly, Connally was LBJ's asshole buddy of long-standing, and his eagerness to kill off the party reform movement represented by McGovern seemed all too obviously hatched with Johnson's—and probably Daley's—tacit approval. Now he appeared in dissenter's robes, abandoning party loyalty out of "principle." McGovern was a danger to America and something had to be done to stop him.

A lot of things made my father mad in those days: Nixon, the war, Daley's Cook County political machine, but something about "Democrats for Nixon" really stuck in his craw, and he launched his own personal counterattack against Connally's slickly produced television ads. Even as McGovern's candidacy plunged, Dad still raised enough money from friends (including a couple of real Republicans) to run an ad in the *Chicago Sun-Times* under the headline "We're Scared, Dick"—alluding to Nixon's penchant for violence

on a grand scale—and now, playing out the string, he was trying hard to keep his boat's boom and mainsail under control in what, after all, is frequently referred to as the Windy City.

But the unruly air currents were the least of the difficulties buffeting well-meaning liberals in November 1972. The fundamental problem was that there were, indeed, many Democrats for Nixon, and all too few Republicans (or anyone else, for that matter) for McGovern. That didn't deter my dad, though, who like so many of his fellow successful Americans, believed deeply in the power of advertising and charade to sway public opinion. It's no coincidence he named our modest cruising yacht *Potemkin*.

Anyhow, as I stood in line to hear McGovern speak, the wait to enter grew longer and longer and I badly needed to urinate. Like all American cities, Chicago has no public restrooms to speak of, but I remembered there was a chemical "head" aboard *Potemkin*. Asking my friends to hold my place in line I raced the half block to Michigan where I sighted my father hanging on to the boom like John Muir clinging to a redwood tree. From the east side of Michigan, I clambered up the trailer and into the cockpit. I hurriedly greeted my dad, who seemed not the least surprised by my sudden appearance, and ducked below deck to use the toilet. The ceiling was too low to permit me to stand, so I knelt and prepared to relieve myself into the pot illuminated only from the exterior by the blue-hued mercury vapor street lights.

It occurred to me that my situation was absurd, or at least as implausible as Republicans for McGovern, that I had no business peeing in a pot on the good ship *Potemkin*. But then again, why not? In many respects it still felt like the Sixties and anything seemed possible, even the election of George McGovern, even ending the nine-year-old war in Vietnam, even urinating on a boat in the middle of Michigan Avenue. I'd almost forgotten I was in Mayor Daley's Chicago.

Then, Bang!, and my idyll shattered in so many tiny yellow droplets. The whole of *Potemkin*'s fiberglass hull shuddered and rocked from the shock of a very great impact. I nearly fell over, bracing myself against the curvature of the hull. Rapidly zipping up, I poked my head out into the cold night air. A northbound city bus had smashed into the boat's boom, bending it and very nearly lifting the boat off the trailer. At first, it seemed odd that the bus driver didn't stop—that he behaved for all the world like a hit and run driver. But quickly my mind cleared. Though my father later insisted it was an accident, I'd begun my political education in earnest that night, and I was learning firsthand how few surprises ever occurred in American politics, and especially in Chicago. Republicans for McGovern, indeed! The bus driver must have done it on purpose, no doubt on direct orders from City Hall!

A ND YET, in that fading moment of American radicalism, there were still some things that escaped the control of the boss of bosses, Mayor Richard J. Daley. Chief among them was the behavior of his most erratic, hot-tempered subordinate, Edward V. Hanrahan, the Cook County state's attorney. Once considered Daley's heir apparent, Hanrahan had blotted his copybook in December 1969 by sending his own policemen (was it only in Chicago that a prosecutor could have his own police force?) to "raid" an apartment occupied by two officials of the Illinois Black Panther Party, Fred Hampton and Mark Clark, allegedly to search for guns. The resulting deaths of the Illinois state Panther chairman and the local leader from Peoria had looked to some people like out-and-out murder, but three years later Hanrahan was hanging tough and, to everyone's amazement, scheduled to appear at the rally that night, side by side with McGovern.

To understand how implausible was Hanrahan's political survival, one must first appreciate the utter imperviousness of Chicago to, shall we say, "openness" over the decades. "Chicago ain't ready for reform yet," one alderman had declared after Richard Daley's election to the mayoralty, and the words still rang true in the immediate aftermath of Hanrahan's buccaneering assault on the Panther apartment in the heart of the West Side's black ghetto. Incarcerating Black Panthers was all the rage in 1969, and the state's attorney's enthusiasm for the task was very much in keeping with mainstream anxiety about this small group of posturing black men possessed of a few guns, a talent for soundbites, and some Gilbert and Sullivan-style party titles. Just the day before the Chicago Panther raid, U.S. Secret Service agents in San Francisco had arrested David Hilliard, the party's "chief of staff," for allegedly

Gibet.

threatening to kill President Nixon in a speech at an anti-war rally.

But nobody died when the Secret Service grabbed Hilliard. In Chicago, Hanrahan's agents left two people dead and then loudly proclaimed that they got what they deserved. In this bloody PR enterprise, the state's attorney was ably assisted by the *Chicago Tribune,* then still the curious creature of the late Colonel Robert McCormick. That the city's political machine was Democratic and its journalistic establishment Republican hardly mattered; the *Tribune* hated all the same people as the Daley machine: longhairs, liberals, communists, feminists, peaceniks, uppity blacks, environmentalists, and intellectuals—perhaps especially intellectuals. In those days, the *Tribune* was not only the self-proclaimed "World's Greatest Newspaper," it was the "American Paper for Americans," a uniquely shrill, self-righteous dealer in the strange fixations of McCormick's homemade brand of right-wing paranoia.

So when the clamor for an independent investigation of Hanrahan's raid grew too loud and persistent, the *Tribune* reacted with characteristic self-confidence. A week after the shootings, on December 11, the paper published its "EXCLUSIVE" account of the raid under a front-page banner headline. "Exclusive" was an apt description: It was a story told exclusively from the point of view of Hanrahan and the fourteen policemen who raided the Panther lair on West Monroe Street. The law enforcement authorities had, of course, behaved honorably and legally throughout the events of that morning, the *Trib* reported. The safety of nearby residents had been fore-most in their minds. "At first I thought we'd hit the place at 8 o'clock that night," Sgt. Daniel Groth told *Tribune* reporters Edward Lee and Robert Weidrich. "But after talking it over, we decided that would be a bad time, both for our safety and that of residents of the area." Sounding a bit like a visiting zoologist, Groth continued, "It's a heavily populated neighborhood… and… we feared such a raid might create an incident in the area, which we knew was the heart of Panther territory. Our object was to avoid an incident." Groth, it seemed, was every inch the community relations officer. But the crucial facts, the ones that supposedly exonerated the cops, were provided by Hanrahan himself. Thus, we learned from the *Tribune,* "Hanrahan… made available official police photographs which they said conclusively proved the Panthers opened the battle by firing a shotgun blast thru [sic] the apartment door." Before long, the story got even more specific, and more exciting, as the lawmen recalled pounding on the door, clearly identifying themselves, and announcing they had a search warrant:

> Then suddenly, as the two policemen entered the anteroom they said a shotgun blast was fired thru the closed living room door, a charge which later proved to have been a solid rifle lead deer slug fired from a twelve-gauge shotgun. The slug pierced the door, ripping splinters from the outside of the door as it exited and narrowly missed the two policemen. Photographs of this door were furnished the *Tribune* by Hanrahan as evidence that the Panthers inside the flat fired the opening shot at his men.

And sure enough, the *Tribune* printed two photos depicting two different views of the same bullet hole and provided a helpful graphic, a neat white circle, to make sure the reader didn't miss the hole and its significance. On a different page, more photos proved that the trigger-happy Panthers had fired first at police entering the back door as well, further justifying the police fusillade.

It wasn't "Dewey Defeats Truman," it was worse. The same day, the leading afternoon paper, the *Chicago Daily News*, reported the interesting fact that none of its reporters could find any evidence that the "deer slug" had damaged the wall behind the front door. This sounded mighty suspicious. What's more, it turned out that that the "bullet holes" in the back door so carefully identi-

Mitrailleuse Hotchkiss.

fied by the *Tribune* were actually rusty nailheads, and a bullet-riddled bathroom door was really a bedroom door. It began to look quite possible that the cops had simply broken in with guns blazing.

The next morning, the *Sun-Times* boldly front-paged Hanrahan's and the rival *Tribune's* shame while *Daily News* columnist Mike Royko piled on with a withering column of his own. Thoroughly humiliated, The World's Greatest Newspaper beat a hasty retreat. Weidrich returned to writing a gossip column and by Saturday the 13th, the paper reported the launching of a federal civil rights investigation into the killings in a story that carried no byline at all. By Sunday, the Panther disaster was off the front page altogether and the *Tribune* was back to doing what it did best, announcing the bracing news that "fifty-two Reds" had been reported killed by U.S. troops near My Lai, site of the famous massacre that

McCormick's successors had been aggressively doubting since the first reports.

But up in the Tribune Tower, management was shaken to its core. Three years later, by the time the bus hit the *Potemkin* on Michigan Avenue, the paper was no longer the "American Paper for Americans" and had even adopted some Frenchified intellectual pretensions. Weidrich's gossip column now appeared on the new "Perspective" page, advertised as "A Forum for Ideas, Analysis, and Diverse Opinions." It must have been tough for Weidrich to swallow his pride after the Panther "exclusive," but to be published directly beneath an epigraph from Voltaire—"I do not agree with a word that you say, but I will defend to the death your right to say it"—must have tasted of the bitterest bile. Col. McCormick's great and preposterous rag—really the world's worst major newspaper—was well on its way to becoming the respectable, diversity-minded corporate citizen that it is today. The current owner of the *Sun-Times*, Conrad Black, today finds himself well to the right of his competitor's bland bureaucracy. Never again will the *Tribune* surprise anyone.

S QUEEZING INSIDE the Auditorium Theater to hear McGovern speak, my friends and I managed to get seats in the first balcony. Thousands of people were left on the street to hear the speeches over loudspeakers. But we weren't the earnest, young crowds who had got "clean for Gene" four years before. The McGovernites of 1972 were more ragged

BALLAD OF SUSAN SMITH

A Modern "Cruel Mother Ballad" to be sung to the tune of
"There was a Lady Living Yore"

I put my car into reverse
On a lee and lonely
This will be my babies' hearse
Down by the green lake side-ee-o

I am a daughter of the Mills
On a lee and lonely
Young I am but doomed to kill
Down by the green lake side-ee-o

I had a love I thought was true
On a lee and lonely
The more he rubbed the redder I grew
Down by the green lake side-ee-o

Left high and dry and all alone
On a lee and lonely
These Babes weigh me down like a stone
Down by the green lake side-ee-o

I see a dark man in my dream
On a lee and lonely
He'll be the one to take the blame
Down by the green lake side-ee-o

in appearance, more divided among ourselves, more into drugs. And unlike the '68ers, we knew we were going to lose. Even the seating at the rally reflected this. Daley had packed the best seats on the orchestra level with ward heelers and left the cheap seats in back and above to the hippies and McGovernites. The mayor had a lively if petty sense of irony: This seating arrangement could only have been revenge for the unceremonious ejection of his delegation at the party convention back in the summer in favor of a delegation led by Jesse Jackson. Now it was the reformers' turn to sit at the back of the bus.

Matt Danaher, Circuit Court clerk and surrogate son to Daley, introduced the boss as "the greatest mayor this country has ever known." Daley approached the podium and took the microphone, or rather seized it and pressed it to the corner of his mouth. Never an accomplished public speaker, Daley was still at his level-headed best, gruffly balancing the absurdly fractured menagerie assembled that night on his home turf. Shaken by the violence of the 1968 Democratic convention, embarrassed by the Panther raid, humiliated at his own party's convention in 1972, stung by independent gubernatorial candidate Dan Walker's upset primary victory a few months before, he was gradually regaining full control of his city.

But the fissures caused by Vietnam and the reform movement were still present. Before Daley came to the podium, Danaher had introduced the entire Cook County Democratic slate, bottom to top, including Hanrahan. Yes, Hanrahan. He had survived indictment, Daley's efforts to dump him from the ticket, and the general outrage of all right-thinking citizens in northeastern Illinois. When he stood to acknowledge Danaher's welcome, the ward heelers rose as one with their organization-printed signs and roared their approval, while the hippies in the cheap seats simultaneously shrieked their deafening boos. Walker, author of the report that called the melee at the '68 convention a "police riot," stood for Hanrahan but refused to applaud as the other candidates had dutifully done.

A brave act by Walker, but clearly the momentum was going the other direction now. Following Hanrahan's cacophonous moment on stage, when all the hopeless contradictions in the Democratic Party became vividly clear, Daley introduced McGovern, in a moment of dispiriting anticlimax, as "The Next President of the United States." The party hacks seated below applauded perfunctorily, but the people in the balcony stood and cheered. I recall feeling some genuine hope then. I didn't realize that the most telling moment had already come, a little earlier when McGovern first entered the theater to thunderous, uninterrupted applause. Several minutes into this astonishing display of emotion, an irritated Danaher had taken the microphone and shouted, with that unmistakable Chicago whine, "Siddown!" And a lot of people did.

O No! O No! What have I done?
On a lee and lonely
To please a man I've killed my sons
Down by the green lake side-ee-o

Naught will cleanse me of this sin
On a lee and lonely
To please myself I'd do it again
Down by the green lake side-ee-o

A Nation's pity for my plight
On a lee and lonely
I look so innocent and white
Down by the green lake side-ee-o

Black Man, Black Man, I accuse you
On a lee and lonely
On Nationwide you'll get your due
Down by the green lake side-ee-o

Why can a woman rout her womb
On a lee and lonely
But not close her babies tomb?
Down by the green lake side-ee-o

My face it cracks at what I say
On a lee and lonely
I'll spend my life in bitter gray
Far from the green lake side-ee-o

You did as much as dash our brains
On a lee and lonely
Blood on your hands is our refrain
Down by the green lake side-ee-o

My Babes! They speak—The cold black lake
On a lee and lonely
Shoots forth its hand, more souls to take
Down by the green lake side-ee-o

—Lee Ann Brown

THE BANALITY OF LEISURE

Karen Olsson

THE LEISURE CLASS is dead: According to a 1999 article in the *New York Times*, even the wealthiest of Manhattan trust fund twentysomethings are seeking gainful employment ("The Rich Find It's Uncool Not to Have a Job," announced the bold type). We are all doing our part for the economy now, helping to run up those productivity numbers. Newspapers have yet to herald a "new frugality" among those with trust funds, however; as luck would have it, our renewed spirit of work is soaring unencumbered by outdated Protestant inclinations toward saving or modest living. By happy coincidence, society's nod of approval these days is going to the well-heeled workaholic, the sort who works hard and spends massively, leading exactly that lifestyle which best serves the interest of capital. It is now fashionable to brag about how much you work *and* to drive a very large car. Leisure itself is declared at risk of extinction, and for many of us the weekend, time which might be dedicated to leisure, is now dedicated to either work or shopping.

It is evidently this recent use of the word "weekend" to mean "time during which you buy things" that the *Wall Street Journal* intended in giving the name "Weekend Journal" to a relatively new section published every Friday. When it comes to coverage of shopping, the Weekend Journal is without rival. Since its inception in the spring of 1998, it has chronicled high-end consumption in astonishing detail, retaining a corps of reporters—*real reporters*—to cover bathroom sinks, new trends in swimming pool design, new trends in swimming pool raft design, throw pillows, art collecting, mansion prices, online sales of wedding gowns, parasailing, monogrammed furniture, luxury box seats at the theater, $200-a-bottle pink champagne—the list could go on and on. Consider the following sentences, excerpted from different Weekend Journal articles:

> Generously proportioned above-the-counter bowls, called "vessels," are taking sinks from ordinary to attention getter.

> Why he had purchased a grand cru Bordeaux is a mystery. Such was not his normal fare.

> We couldn't even go to the best beaches; for two days, hundreds of protesters with loudspeakers blocked access to them.

Karen Olsson is a co-editor of the *Texas Observer*.

The W Hotel's Heartbeat restaurant in
New York has a "tea sommelier" to help
guests pick the right brew.

THE SECTION'S WEALTH of data on conspicuous consumption, its front-lines
reporting on the bizarre and complex
sport of turn-of-the-millennium acquisi-
tion, can be overwhelming at times. The
leisure class may be on its last legs, but the
term Thorstein Veblen once used to describe the spending practices of that
class, "conspicuous consumption," has
not lost its relevance. In fact consumption seems to be getting more conspicuous all the time.

There's a whole lot of shopping going
on, and trailing along in its wake is an
unprecedented amount of analysis of
shopping. The sort of inspection of material culture that Veblen pioneered has
become increasingly common. While the
spending binge of the early to mid-Eight-
ies was, at least in the popular mind,
largely about upper class extravagance
(mythologized in fictions like *Bonfire of
the Vanities* and *Dynasty*), more recent
consumption is about the broader "upper-
middle class's" expanding list of must-
buys, available for sale at the Pottery Barn
and Williams-Sonoma and Stuff.com,
and a growing fascination with the entire
cycle of marketing and buying. Instead
of nighttime soaps about the superrich
we now have *New Yorker* articles about
Restoration Hardware and "Nobrow Culture." And every Friday, the Weekend
Journal, which is so much more than just
Consumer Reports for the people who fly
business class. In addition to movie and
book reviews and feature articles on
lifestyle topics (such as finding doctors,
masseuses, and music teachers who do

house visits in order to save on drive
time), the Journal publishes a full page of
opinion pieces on cultural matters. By this
I do not mean that the Weekend Journal
weighs in on, say, controversies over history textbooks or theories of conceptual
art. No, in the world of the Weekend Journal, consumer culture *is* the culture. This
central fact is coyly presented: The ironic
style prevails in the articles, verging at
times on self-parody—which is of course
a means of tacitly acknowledging the
shallowness of the subject and the silliness
of writing about it, while proceeding to
do so anyway. As such, it presents not just
the fancy pillow but a glimpse into the
psychology of fancy-pillow buying, and a
general endorsement of the idea that one
might devote considerable thought and
energy to the pillow hunt.

IT WAS VEBLEN who pointed out, in *The
Theory of the Leisure Class*, his 1899
treatise on the psychology of consuming,
that consumption occupies a central place
not just in the economy, but in the heads
of status-minded people, wealthy people
in particular. What those people bought
depended on what other people bought,
for humans are given to comparing and
competing with one another. (He called
this "invidious comparison.") For Veblen,
consumption was all about demonstrat-
ing your rank, a "symbolic display of mastery" in a society that no longer afforded
its status-seeking members very many
opportunities for literal shows of prowess—which had been more plentiful in
the days of soldiering and estate-holding.
Status-minded consumption reflected the
anonymity of urban life: In village society, Veblen argued, thrift was honored

over wasteful display, since everyone already more or less knew what everyone else had. The values placed on prowess and thrift didn't disappear in capitalist society, but they did become secondary to the demands of invidious comparison—rating one's fellow Americans based on what they own. You may not be able to go *mano a mano* with your neighbor, but you can have better topiary.

Veblen's star, never terribly high to begin with, fell as the idea of a "leisure class" dominated by Captains of Industry faded—and as the political and literary movements that informed his work, Midwestern Populism and naturalism, disappeared. By midcentury, those sharp-edged prairie philosophies had given way to moderate social science: In 1953 David Riesman would write, in a book on Veblen, that "save in Texas ... the crazy millionaire is dead, and a subdued nonconspicuousness seems to be spreading over our leisure and consumption practices." Veblen's analysis of spending was declared irrelevant because the spenders had changed, and even Riesman's well-to-do Harvard students were wearing blue jeans. But the disappearance of the old leisure class doesn't diminish Veblen's primary insight that spending money is intimately linked to being visible as a spender and to watching others spend—and that this is especially evident among people who have a lot of money to begin with.

Since Veblen's day, the great surge of mass consumerism has naturally altered the spending landscape; by the time Nixon showed our kitchens to the Russians, conspicuous consumption had be-

come a national pastime. "Symbolic mastery" was supplanted by "keeping up with the Joneses," and then, as Juliet Schor has noted, by "keeping up with the cast of *Friends.*" While the tendency toward invidious comparison lives on, we're increasingly uncertain who to compare ourselves to, and increasingly likely to look to the richer-than-average sorts portrayed in magazines and movies and TV shows. Add to that the presumptive predicament of many *Wall Street Journal* readers: They've recently made small killings in the stock market. They feel a little weird about having all this money all of a sudden, and they don't know what to spend it on. Vacations? Cars? Jennifer Aniston's pants?

Soothing the anxieties of the shopper-reader is a curious and subtle art. For one thing, the shopper-reader should be made to feel well off, but not too rich—a principle evidenced by the use of democratic phrases like "the rest of us" and humble-sounding assertions about what "average" means. "Forget the Malibu beach house, the Aspen condo, and the Martha's Vineyard bungalow," advised an article on "Second Homes for the Rest of Us." "With prices in the traditional second-home communities soaring through the roof, savvy house hunters are finding great deals in up-and-coming getaway spots from Belize to West Virginia." (Other "up-and-coming" spots where "the rest of us" might find bargain second homes, according to the article, include Nevada, Crete, and Thailand—a 2-1 condo on the island of Phuket can be had for a measly $174,000.)

Not all the Journal's normative invocations are so blatantly silly; more typical is the average-shopper allusion made in a piece on the "The New Narcissism" in furniture design. According to the article, although most people won't be buying the baronial dining table (seats twenty-four) exhibited at last year's International Fine Art & Antique Show, that table and everything else at the show are indicators of "current trends in the high-end market—trends that, knocked-off and reinterpreted cheaply, end up in the average American home a year or two later, sold by chains like ABC Carpet & Home, Pier One Imports, and Pottery Barn." From Joe Six-Pack to Joe Pottery Barn: By defining average up, the Journal lets its readers know that they're normal.[†] In addition to being reassured that luxury goods are no longer emblems of snobbery, Weekend Journal shopper-readers are also told over and over again that they won't be laughed at by the salespeople: Just because you don't know too much about wine and art doesn't mean you can't be a savvy consumer of either. In accomplishing this crucial task of journalism, no part of the section has been more reliable than "Tastings," the weekly wine column by Dorothy J. Gaiter and John Brecher (*Wall Street Journal* editors who are married to one another). In a series of vinous adventures, intrepid tasters Gaiter and Brecher find good wines, and bargain good wines, at every turn.

While each week's dispatch is usually accompanied by a list of the wines discussed, a good many of the columns end by reminding the reader that, while these particular wines may not be available in your area, the important thing is to try, say, an Australian chardonnay, or an $80-per-person winemaker's dinner.

The flushed proselytizing sentiment of "Tastings" is of course seconded by the ads that surround it. *Go ahead, pronounce it 'peanut nor.' We'll still love you,* reads an ad for the "Virtual Vineyards" website, expertly flattering "you" (that is, assuming that "you" know what pinot noir is, and how to pronounce it) while disavowing snobbishness at the same time. This doesn't just happen on the wine page: Indeed, the apparent similarities, in subject and spirit, between the advertising and the articles throughout the entire section might well lead one to mistake the Weekend Journal for one big advertising vehicle. But it's not quite that, since the articles work far better than the ads, in terms of persuasion and selling. Once you've read over a whole list of wines along with their ratings and prices, you're already shopping. The accompanying article tells you it's okay to be shopping, and *then* you're really ready for Virtual Vineyards.

THE MOST OBVIOUS tension in the Weekend Journal's *buy! buy! buy!* approach comes through its stark contrast with the traditional conservatism of its

---

[†] It almost goes without saying that this recalibration requires forgetting about the working class. The Weekend Journal itself made that explicit, in a September 3 column by *Wall Street Journal* editorial board ingenue Amity Shlaes. Entitled "Blue Collar Man Endangered in Age of New Work," it began with the sentence, "Today, we e-workers have a hard time even remembering the purpose of Labor Day," and went on to celebrate a brave new post-labor world.

parent, the *Wall Street Journal*. As members of that newspaper's editorial board have amply demonstrated, it's not hard to be a free-marketeer and a moralizer at the same time, but the Weekend Journal's open-wallet ethos is not quite compatible with the righteous-'n'-godly variety of conservativism. It's hard to maintain that simple hedonism is what John Calvin, John Locke, and the Framers had in mind. And bridging this divide is where the Weekend Journal has done its most valuable service. On the most superficial level, the Weekend Journal reconciles shopping and tory values by distinguishing (and celebrating) acceptable, savvy consuming from the sea of crass, low-rent consuming that is said to surround us. A column from October 1999, for instance, denounced the T-shirts being sold at New York's Metropolitan Museum of Art in conjunction with an exhibit of Ingres portraits, and then went on to denounce the rise of museum merchandise in general, which, writer Eric Gibson complained, commercializes and trivializes art. Even though the Weekend Journal publishes pieces about buying and selling art every week—even though it's just fine for art itself, not to mention other auctioned items written about in the Journal, like Hindu religious objects and Allen Ginsberg's medic-alert bracelet, to be put on the block—the selling of Ingres T-shirts is an indication of how tainted by consuming our culture has become. "With two sets of values in close proximity—those of the marketplace and those of high culture—there needs to be some

sort of standard in place to harmonize them," sniffs Gibson.

Lots of luck, "high culture." That such a contention comes in a publication whose coverage of art is coverage of the art marketplace seems to have disturbed no one. Perhaps this is because the Weekend Journal does make an effort to do some of this harmonizing—to insist that good taste and the market can reign peacefully side by side. The last page of every edition features opinions, signed and unsigned—as well as a big advertisement, often for Armani—under the heading "Taste." Here the shopper-reader is treated to a variety of meditations, on such questions as: Is the auctioning of Marilyn Monroe's personal effects a "good idea"? (Not particularly.) Can creative writing be taught? (No.) Is family-friendly television programming on the rise? (Maybe.) Should a church in Minneapolis have defended a parishioner who was once a member of the Symbionese Liberation Army? (No way, and the fact that it did proves that most churches today are nothing but redoubts of therapeutic feel-goodism.)

"Taste" is a useful device for the Weekend Journal's uneasy balancing act. When confronted by any objection to consuming other than one rooted in the shifting sands of fashion, the Weekend Journal sees red. Reviewing an anthology of essays critical of current consumer patterns, writer Daniel Akst referred to its authors as "the indulgence police," and pointed out (zap!) that a lot of them are themselves quite well off. For Akst, the crucial matter was the right of prosperous people—now cruelly under attack—to buy whatever they want. In the last paragraph he acknowledged that the current consuming culture is not entirely without fault, "yet even our most ardent scolds aren't moving into mud huts in search of answers, and who can blame them? Personally, I plan to think about it in the Jacuzzi."

Short of moving into a mud hut, there's no escape from the consumer culture, and unless you're willing to do that, the Weekend Journal argues, critical examination is nothing but hypocrisy. Naturally the section does not bother to consider the origins of all those consumer goods contained within its pages, or the consequences of development on the island of Phuket, much less the necessity of actually acquiring monogrammed furniture or Hindu statuary or what have you. Of course not: *Leave that sort of thing to the indulgence police. We're just having some fun here.*

At times the fun can get to be too much. To view the world as first and foremost a consumer is to cheerfully strap on an enormous pair of intellectual blinders, such as writer Nancy Keates must have worn while penning an article on "The Five Worst Vacations." In it, Keates traveled to places which, because of political or environmental problems, make for lousy vacation spots—like the Falkland Islands, Asbestos, Quebec, and Vieques,

Puerto Rico, an island where U.S. Navy pilots practice dropping bombs. In April of 1999, an errant U.S. bomb (off target by nearly two miles) killed a Puerto Rican guard and, what a bummer, the locals were upset about this at the time Keates and an unnamed companion visited. She ended her article by describing an encounter with a tourist from Memphis, "desperately trying to navigate her way through the placard-wielding protesters. Finally, she gave up with a frustrated cry: 'This is terrible!' " Continues the writer, "We couldn't have put it better ourselves."

And this perhaps suggests why the "Taste" page's attempts to navigate the culture for the benefit of rich turn-of-the-millennium consumers seem so weirdly flatfooted—because all that consuming soon starts to propose a worldview of its own, a will to dumbness that sees the world as just an entertainment provider, a producer of luxury products, a more or less attractive vacation spot. We are all conspicuous consumers, now more than ever, navigating our way through annoying but incomprehensible obstacles like politics or traffic jams, trying to get to the beach. Not that I want to be too dour about this, and ruin all the fun. Did I mention the nifty canvas-and-bamboo, batik-pattern beach umbrella you can buy online? Folded up, it's just about the size of a service baton. Works great for beating back protesters.

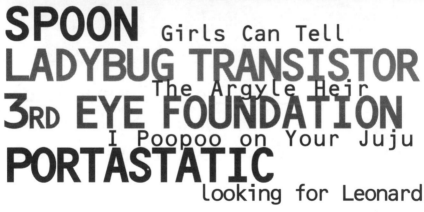

HEATHER

Christopher Sorrentino

THE DAY MY FATHER told me he was leaving for China he found me sitting on the back steps digging my toe into the dirt and playing with an errant stick I'd found far from whatever tree had rejected it. Twelve was my age. We were reading *Johnny Tremaine* in school and dominating the Central Valley's junior field hockey circuit. My instincts were on-target, my reflexes sharp. I smacked a pebble out of my toe's path with the stick. My father was red-faced and flustered.

"Swing you in the tire swing, Skip?"

"Sure," I said. "'Off' to 'China'?"

"Don't make fun."

"You don't know anybody there."

"How do you know? Pishergeh."

"What do you need to go for, anyway."

"You know what, Heather-girl? You're getting big and kicking balls all over the place and meeting the inevitable boys, which is another kettle of fish altogether. Each is a nothing person is what he is— but that's neither here nor there, though even if it were both or either of those places it wouldn't be as if you ever paid me any mind, so why bother? It's fine, I'm old, what do I know? But still, what I say is 'Don't kid yourself that your dreams'll be around for you, Heather. Five years I give it, tops, five big years, just long enough to utterly and completely ruin your life, and when you come crawling back on your hands and knees through the garbage-strewn streets of the slum you settled into for your squalid life, probably carrying your babies on your back like a poopoose or like a possum or suchlike, you know what? I'll be gone: since your mother pooped out on the marriage, Fresno's been a big rainy parade for me, and besides I have an old man's increasing interest in a gentle climate, a few swaying palms, and a good healthy tan, and the maximum amount of contact I'll want with a burdensome adult daughter, as these twilight years approach and overtake me and eventually conspire to put me in my grave, is a brief and loving and stress-free weekly telephone conversation.' That's what I say. Go ahead and tell me I'm crazy, I'm boring. Nice, very nice from a daughter to whom attention is paid and things are provided. But I'm open. Even now, a successful adult person like myself who influences the minds of the young is always looking for a little honest criticism, looking to you for that. So I'll be seeing you."

Christopher Sorrentino is the author of *Sound on Sound* (Dalkey Archive). His new novel is scheduled to be published by Farrar, Straus & Giroux.

This was Dad's valedictory address: He took off toward the Buick Somerset and the next I heard he'd cleaned out his office at Fresno State and gone AWOL.

I stayed for a while at the home of Cindy T. It was she who taught me the skill for which I've gained such backyard renown here in Southern California. We practiced on Mr. T's rinsed out "long neck" deposit bottles in the shed behind her ranch house in Clovis. We climbed from her bedroom window down the drainpipe at night and went to the cowboy bars to stand in the parking lots and watch the men stagger out and fire up the engines of their awesome, dust-covered machines.

Mr. T taught gym. He wore a whistle. No, he wasn't the pervert you're hoping for, but he was, alas, a bore. He read aloud to us from Hemingway. Not even the short stories: *Death in the Afternoon*. "If he was one he should redeem, for the tribe, the prissy exhibitionistic, aunt-like, withered old maid moral arrogance of a Gide; the lazy, conceited debauchery of a Wilde who betrayed a generation; the nasty, sentimental pawing of humanity of a Whitman and all the mincing gentry. Viva El Greco El Rey de los Maricónes."

"What's that mean, Mr. T?"

"What it means is King of the Faggots, girls."

"Not that. The old maid pawing stuff."

"Oh. That. Um."

JOHNNY TREMAINE underwent a painful operation and the book ended.

"There was NO ANESTHETIC back then, kids. That's the significance," said Mr. Walsh, our English teacher. "NO anesthetic. NONE. Johnny is going to have the tender flesh of his maimed hand separated from itself with his eyes WIDE OPEN. It will SMART. Who can tell me WHY he is doing this? WHY would he undergo this ordeal? WHY? Anybody?"

I VISITED our old house in the "faculty ghetto" to watch it fall into disrepair. The yard and grounds remained the same, having been cemented over some time before, and shone like mica in the heat, but the house itself began to fall apart. The mail brought no news from China. Then Mr. T died in one of the many tule fog accidents on 99 we accepted as a grim fact of life in Raisin Country. Mrs. T said she couldn't afford another mouth to feed, and Cindy T had become kind of a bore anyway, so I packed my bag. No hard feelings. Mrs. T read at the funeral: "He lives in a country with as severe a climate as any that is farmed, but it is a very healthy country; he has food, wine, his wife and children, or he has had them, but he has no comfort, nor much capital, and these possessions are not ends in themselves; they are only a part of life and life is something that comes before death." Wandering the air-conditioned aisles of APPLIANCE SUPERSAVINGS WORLD! after the funeral, it occurred to me that this was a message Fresno might not have received clearly. Then a man leaped out at me so suddenly his little acetate necktie actually moved, albeit stiffly.

"Pretty girl, hold this. Stand right by this display of motor oil with a smile on that fresh-from-the-farm face and hold this up with the label out."

He was a Sales Manager and I was in no mood for trouble.

WE BEGAN TO READ a new book in school. Since it was actually an Honors Class it was a contemporary book. It was called *Plummer's Crossing* by Hannah Trost Beckhorn. "I know this: Vast as it is, that rolling plain isn't big enough to hide one's heart in."

Here's the ironic thing: It's this book exactly that's been adapted for the movie they've "tentatively" cast me in. It's a lame book, but I know all the girls from school will probably run out to see the movie because we read it way back when. I'm supposed to play the part of Jane. Here's the story: Three sisters, Kate, Anne, and Jane Plummer, are reunited on the family farm in the hamlet of Plummer's Crossing when their father, Conroy, falls off a ladder. In the hospital for the ladder business he's diagnosed as having had a stroke and he lies there blinking yes or no to everything with the one good eye on his crooked face ("the texture and quality of old putty ..."). Mom's history, incidentally. Kate has moved to Chicago where she's become an options hustler. She's very strong-willed and is always pulling out a cellular phone. No farming for her. Anne stayed on the farm, which she works in addition to the land owned by her drunk husband, Kevin. Bitter is her middle name. Creditors and patched dresses. I, Jane, the baby, am studying in New York to be a writer. My boyfriend the law student (glasses, Jewish-looking) shows up in the beginning and asks Jeez, Kiddo, What Do You Want To Go Back To The Sticks For? and I know it's all over between us. I sort of cry as my United flight taxis from the jetway, then I resolutely put on my funky downtown glasses and open my fat book. All sorts of things happen, we fight constantly, reveal unknown things about ourselves, and then there's a big rainstorm. The crops get washed right out of their furrows and the cows all drown, except old Floss. "Well," says Anne, pulling on her gumboots, "that's a start." Anyway, principal photography on this great American saga begins in Toronto later this year.

I had myself declared an emancipated minor and moved into Mrs. Falajian's Boarding House. After school I worked for Mr. Phrifter (the Sales Manager) at APPLIANCE SUPERSAVINGS WORLD!

"Hold it higher, honey. That's right, right next to your budding geniuses there. When those boys come up with that moony zit-faced look they have just sell yourself and the product will follow."

I thought of myself as Orphan Annie, that cryptic figure of self-reliance, displacing Death from his familiar place in the world's shadows and ditches, under its eaves. "Daddy" placed me in the care of Punjab and the Asp and we somehow just got separated. "Leapin' lizards, Mr. Phrifter, we sold out th' whole warehouse!" "Arf!"

One day, I received a postcard at Mrs. Falajian's. The picture was of the main street of Porterville, taken long ago judging from the dress of the pedestrians and the style of the cars parked by the curb, and it had been postmarked there as well. It read:

> China is great. More here than I knew. Plate depicts old Shinto garden where rhymes still beloved by children were composed with the most delicate care. China's my soul mate! Yours, Daddy.

He had drawn a little yin-yang symbol next to his signature.

I thought about the postcard for a long time after that. It didn't stop me in my tracks, or anything. Porterville was of course the home of the Tulare County General Hospital, but it was also a pleasant enough town in which to establish one's own China in a pinch. Then, one night, I was reading one of my favorite books in bed: the Time-Life Library's *Spies and Spying*. It had been a rough day at the trade shows—I'd since moved on in my career to Valley Thresher, Inc.— midterms were past, and I just wanted to relax with a little esoterica about miniature cameras, pistols concealed in gloves, dead men floating off the coast of Spain carrying written wishes for sardines, and the like. Suddenly, I came across the section on cryptography and its anecdote of a postcard, sent from a Japanese prisoner of war camp, written in *null code:* the recipient in such instances is to disregard, according to a pattern, certain of the letters or words in the message to read its true meaning. In a thrill of understanding, I removed my father's postcard from the bulletin board over my bed and laid the edge of the book over it, moving the book slowly to the right.

China
Plate
rhymes
with
mate!

What was I going to do with that? It sounded like a line from a jumprope song.

VERY FEW INDIVIDUALS ever actually buy a combine. They mutely witness it sitting in its latent splendor, much in the way that Muscovites must have watched the subtle displays of absolute power put on for their benefit during May Day parades. What happens at a combine exhibition is that the equipment is transported to some fairgrounds someplace, and then over the course of a weekend thousands of farmers, their wives, and their children travel there to imagine it chewing up crops. There are usually other diversions as well: a tractor pull or demolition derby, a ferris wheel, concession booths serving that sort of American tempura that rebels in your stomach for days, and strange events that play themselves out using the region's natural abundance of food: One deadly hot day dozens of migrant workers labored to tear thousands of heads of lettuce apart and throw the leaves into an empty above-ground pool that had been brought to the exhibition. After the pool had been filled, helicopters carrying tubs of vinaigrette hovered overhead and dumped their payloads into it. The newspapers and local television gleefully reported the construction of the World's Largest Salad, and the story attracted national attention. The salad wilted in the sun.

But the combines are the main attraction. I would circle the combine, slowly, telling my (its) audience stories about it, like a docent. I tried for that, anyway. I didn't want it to sound like I was rattling off facts, but revealing studied opinions. Other times, I'd pose on one of its gigantic tires, usually in a swimsuit, submitting to hundreds of photographs. People would come up and ask me if they could touch it—that is, the combine. I felt as if I'd unlocked the emotional power of the machine. My peroration: "Without it, there's no bread on the nation's tables. There's no grain for the hungry of the world." That was when I began to think about acting.

If you're from a small town and interested in getting out you'll understand the allure of "China." You'll understand if you have watched people on a Saturday night getting dressed to go to the cocktail lounge at the Visalia Holiday Inn.

"Sure are some nice folks there, Sandy. But I guess we'll have t' be movin' along."

"Arf!"

NONPROFIT WORKPLACE MINISTRY CONTINUES "CRUSADE AGAINST CRABBINESS AT WORK."

Vernon, CT (3/14/01)—The second annual *Joy at Work Week* ® will be held on April 8-15, 2001. The event is sponsored by Northeast Christians at Work, an all-volunteer group of Christian laypeople who are seeking to reduce workplace stress, crabbiness, and violence by encouraging Godly attitudes and behavior at work.

According to Northeast Christians at Work founder and president Drew Crandall, *Joy at Work Week* ® is timed to coincide with the week between Palm Sunday and Easter. "During this special week," says Crandall, "millions of Protestant and Catholic Americans will celebrate Christ's sacrifice and resurrection. We are issuing a global challenge for Christians to export the joy of their salvation to their workplaces. If we really believe what we say we believe, then we should be the happiest employers and employees on earth."

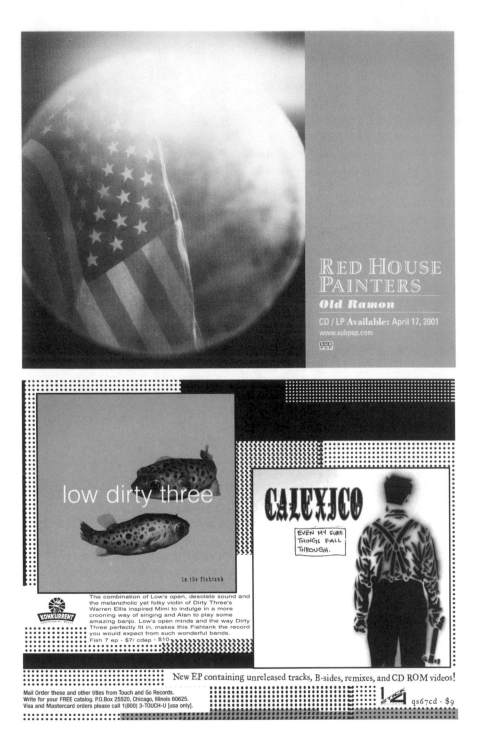

FEAR AND LOFTING
IN A SILICON BOOMTOWN

Martha Bridegam

I LOST A PRETTY TYPICAL argument a while ago with a security manager at San Francisco Centre Mall. The guards had just thrown out a scraggly couple rather than let them use the bathroom. The manager stuck to his three-word explanation: "They're not shopping." Not much I could say. Class discrimination mostly isn't against the law.

So, OK, he probably thought the couple just wanted privacy to shoot up. And being a block from Sixth Street he may have had a point. But if I know San Francisco, the actual and unforgivable sin for which this man and woman were cast out was in fact Not Shopping.

Someday soon they'll give San Franciscans little boxes like parking meters to carry around—sleek black plastic items designed at a dot-com right here and built by people making three bucks a day in Jalisco. Buy something and you get credit on your Residency Meter. If you don't buy something on a given day, you can have a fee deducted from your credit balance. If you don't have credit you can feed it quarters. Or, if you stop spending entirely, the meter radios the cops and they pack you off to Oakland for Not Shopping.

Space has always been valuable in San Francisco, which has water on three sides and no room for sprawl. But during the dot-com gold rush—which I'm happy to be discussing in the past tense—it got as money-pressured as a Beverly Hills gourmet supermarket, with every item required to earn its shelf space.

Now the real estate market is slacking, and some of the dot-commers are falling off their high shelves, but that doesn't make it any easier for the rest of us to hang on. Better pay your rent, keep shopping, and no extra credit for those flowers in your hair. Part of the reason is that, like many American cities, we are experiencing what Patricia Williams calls "white reflux." But here in particular the white middle class has colonized our inner city at T1 speed thanks to the silicon bubble.

Our local history offers some lessons on the subject of gold, silver, and other rushes: Paydirt is not guaranteed. Plenty of miners lose their shirts. The surest way to success isn't hunching over a sluice box all day; it's selling things to those miners who get lucky, or selling the possibility of luck to hopeful investors. Look how Wells Fargo outlived the Wild West and the Hearsts outlasted the Comstock Lode.

Martha Bridegam is a lawyer and freelance writer in San Francisco.

INVISIBLE HAND JOB

Sandy Zipp

Years from now, the most memorable aspect of our late technology bubble will likely be the palaver. Whether all the hot air pumped up the bubble or the bubble inspired the grandiose talk, our age will be forever be remembered for the honking load of bushwa Americans swallowed, at least for a while. There was the overheated futurism of *Being Digital*, and the self-evident absurdity of *Dow 36,000*. And, of course, there was *Wired* magazine, which liked to call itself the "real-time nervous system of the planet."

Ah, *Wired*. In the heady fall of 1996—just as that fabled dot-com brush fire was kicking up—I was a three-day-a-week intern for HotWired, the magazine's Web appendage. I was *there*, man, even if I was virtually invisible. And (to cop a phrase from Walt Whitman) I, too, suffered. When I wasn't ducking Nerf rockets, I was the help-boy for the politics "channel," The Netizen. I pored through pages of wannabe gonzo libertarianism and self-righteous sermonizing about the wonders of new media, chasing down facts on telecommunications law, cryptography politics, and net pornography scares. In my entire nine-month stay in this high-tech romper room I learned how to do maybe three things with HTML. Still, that eclectic "synergy" the magazine incessantly crowed about was crackling. They were "ramping up" all manner of new projects at HotWired: a television show, a web news bureau, a digital art gallery, an interactive lounge party. They were opening up a book publishing company

Now it's the loft-happy San Francisco Residential Builders' Association developers—the ones who sold their buildings in time, anyway—who can walk away with cash, not unvestable stock options. Our rising tide has sunk a lot of boats—if you don't believe me, step down to the courthouse and watch the landlords evict rent-controlled tenants so they can welcome techno-yuppies instead.

My husband Joel and I occupy temporary shelf space in a drafty but picturesque flat South of Market (that's "SoMa" to your real estate agent). We never exactly lived on Planet Dot-Com. Joel "really" does math; I've been mixing legal aid with journalism. But he does work as a programmer and we do live in San Francisco. So we've ended up in frequent participant-observer contact with San Francisco's new society.

We nearly lost our shelf space summer before last when we were both looking for work, and that was probably a typical 1999 San Francisco experience. Everyone was nervous then, and trying not to want stability too badly. My homeless or hotel-hopping clients who learned to travel light and not ask too much; our own yuppie semi-poverty, short of cash and charging goat cheese on the credit card; Joel's job interviews at startups where the coders had stock tickers on the corners of their screens.

You would think the programmers were best off in this picture—and yes, they probably were. But then there was the dot-com man at a party just before the Nasdaq crash who cringed when I wondered what his company did. "Don't ask," he said. "We don't make anything, we don't sell anything." They turned out to run a variation on the Green Stamps gimmick: Shop in certain places, get points toward a prize. He was one of his own customers and had just collected a DVD machine as a Free Gift. I asked what distinguished his company from Amway. He said Amway had products.

Jack London knew SoMa as "South of the Slot." A hundred years ago this was the city's main working-class district, named after the pair of cable car "slots" that ran down Market Street. Now London's Third Street birthplace is on prime dot-com real estate, more a development campus than a public urban space.

We live on the less fashionable end of SoMa, near shelters, sweatshops, a detox center, and a welfare office. But our neighborhood has been forcibly yuppified by big-box loft

developers over the last few years. For a while we had three construction projects on our block alone. Our apartment could rent for half again what we're paying. We're only living in San Francisco at all thanks to rent control and relaxed landlords.

Of course, the twenty-year resident next door reminds us that we're colonists, too—a white, middle-class boy/girl couple in a neighborhood that had been low-rent since the Gold Rush and that, when he moved here, was home mainly to Filipino immigrants and gay men. Folsom Street—just around the corner—was once known for its gay bathhouses. There are still enough leather shops to shock out-of-town visitors, and the Folsom Street Fair draws thousands of bare chests (and other parts) every September. But lively as it remains, this neighborhood is full of ghosts. We newcomers live on earth scorched by AIDS and gentrification.

WE SPENT the last few hours of July 1999 helping a couple in the next alley to clean out their apartment for a midnight eviction deadline. Another "owner move-in" on a rent-controlled unit. They had invited us to a ten o'clock pizza and beer farewell, but when we showed up with part of a six-pack they were still frantically packing the truck. Lots of friends and neighbors pitched in—as many as ten people working at various times. We were not actually done when the landlord and his lawyer appeared at midnight, but they found an angry, sleep-deprived tenant surrounded by

and a British edition of the magazine. New digital identities and cyborg lifestyles were coalescing before one's very eyes.

But even my outmoded Second Wave mind could tell, not long after I got there, that the place was heading for trouble. When things went to pieces, it happened slowly, over the course of a few months. But to those who cared it must have felt sudden, like getting gut-punched. First, Wired Ventures couldn't drum up enough "investor confidence" on Wall Street, and the much-anticipated IPO tanked. Wired TV bombed. Wired Books slowly disappeared, and apparently the Brits just weren't having their "digital revolution" yet. People started to leave or were let go. Soon it was like Saigon in '75, with staffers muttering in the elevators about getting out before the shit really hit the fan. At the Netizen, we went from a high of three or four articles a day during the election to one, maybe two by the first months of 1997. Six months or so after I, too, went on my way, the higher-ups called for the head of the magazine's founder. A few months later, the gates burst open and the wolves rushed in. *Wired* became just another line on chief investor Condé Nast's balance sheet, with new hand-picked New York editors.

This series of disasters also showed just how far ahead of the curve the dispossessed founders of *Wired* were, how far out of the box they could think. Punished by the very market discipline they extolled, the magazine's visionaries at least had the good fortune of taking their medicine years before it was too late to sell out. As for their visions, well, these days they might be a little embarrassing to recall.

Many of these follies are ably catalogued in Paulina Borsook's *Cyberselfish: A Critical Romp Through the Terribly Libertarian Culture of High Tech* (Public

Affairs, 1999). Borsook, a *Wired* dissident and Silicon Valley gadfly, has made a career illuminating the colossal hypocrisy at the heart of "high-tech's default political culture of libertarianism." She is not the first to point it out, of course, but the entire computer industry, particularly those sectors responsible for creating the Internet, are the benificiaries of immense federal subsidies, preferences, and collaboration. The microcomputer is a direct descendant of R&D carried out by the cold war military-industrial complex; the Internet is a tricked-out version of a government research project called Arpanet. "Silicon Valley" as an idea and a place is largely a product of intensive government investment in California's technology industries and public education in the decades following World War II.

Yet by now much of the aerospace industry has fled the state, and the property tax revolt of the Seventies has slowly eroded the state's education system. So it's easy for digital libertarians to imagine that their brave new world has sprung up unaided by anything but their own grit and daring. Regulation is anathema to these worthies—unless you're talking about home-owner mortgage subsidies, single-family building codes, or exclusionary zoning. In fact, Borsook reminds us that without government support for basic infrastructure—roads, water, power, parks, education, the middle-class home mortgage industry—the supposedly placeless cyber-yuppie would be hard-pressed to water the lawn of her postmodern Los Altos hacienda.

Borsook does a serviceable job dissecting the various strains of high-tech libertarianism. There is the free-market fetish-mongering of *Wired*, which sold techno-utopianism as a liberatory lifestyle to an audience of "radical

lots of friends, including some large guys moving furniture and two small middle-class women spouting legalese. They dropped the settlement check and left in a hurry.

A small victory, but then again, when the whole neighborhood helped out in the Depression it was sometimes to move the furniture back indoors in defiance of the sheriff. We've lowered our standards.

The legal aid office where I volunteer sees no letup in the eviction rate, and has itself been displaced by a dot-com. Landlords of rent-controlled properties are jumping on late rent payments. "Nuisance" evictions, for supposed bad conduct, are up. Citywide, Section 8 public housing certificates are expiring for lack of landlords willing to accept subsidized tenants. In mid-June last summer, 5,700 people applied for a chance at fifty-four new units of public housing.

Under Highways 80, 101, and 280, "property sweeps" have turned camping from a difficult but possible way of life for homeless San Franciscans into a risky last resort. A "property sweep" happens when city or highway maintenance crews, acting on police orders, remove the entire contents of a campsite. The crews are supposed to save any items of value for later collection by the owners. In practice the crusher trucks often eat sleeping bags and raingear, medicine and eyeglasses.

Sweeps are especially common in India Basin, under and around Highway 280. (This is the scenic Jag-laden route to San Jose.) The Residential Builders Association pushed through permits to build lofts all over India Basin, which has long been a live-and-let-live warehouse district full of rusty truck parts and wild fennel. The inhabitants still include bikers, hippies, artists, mechanics, and metal recyclers, many of them proudly self-sufficient "vehicular residents." Now that the district has to be made safe for yuppification, the law in its majestic equality is sweeping campers out of the freeway's wide rain shadow, and sending city tow crews to take cars, trucks and campers from people who use them as their homes.

This notion of clearing, paving over and repopulating jibes eerily with the newly rehabilitated word "solutions." Hitler couldn't put that word out of fashion forever. High-tech copywriters love it. A company down the street from us is typical: "DigitalThink: The Internet Learning Solution."

Joel was scoped by two software companies with names in the "_____ Solutions" format and another that uses "solution" in the name of a major product. One company uses the slogan: "Dynamic, Smart, Connected. Embedded Databases and Development Solutions."

The "solutions" phrase also extends into local politics—as does its unrealistic promise of breakthrough quick fixes. In his 1999 campaign, mayoral candidate Clint Reilly put out a campaign booklet called "Homeless Solutions," promoting something called "compassionate refusal."

Of course a lot of the money is in solutions to problems that had to be invented first. Like one company's work on Internet surfing machines for exercise treadmills.

Joel interviewed at one company that builds solutions involving narking appliances. A low, new building slabbed out into the bay mud where the employees have to open a door with their security badges every time they go to the bathroom. They talked about washing machines that analyze their own problems and call the lonely repairman themselves. Also, toilets that test your waste products and, if necessary, call your doctor. (Or why not your parole officer?)

Joel had another interview at a dot-com startup near a brewery, in one of San Francisco's fashionably post-industrial bonanza districts. Internet finance solutions this time around. The programmers there kept boasting about their "informal atmosphere" and the beer keg in the kitchen. One claimed the keg had helped his headache problem. The

individualists," ready to express themselves through Palm Pilots, virtual erotica, and web-shopped home-delivered gourmet meals. (Does anyone wonder why Condé Nast bought the magazine out?) Borsook breaks down the pseudo-science of "bionomics," an outdated mess of second-rate speculations about the equivalencies between nature and economics. The free market is just like a rain forest, goes the thinking behind this collection of fatuous conceits. Markets move and grow with the same complex ecology as a high-canopy ecosystem. Of course, market ideals won't soon "evolve" to the point where they no longer drive corporations to plow under acre after acre of actual rain forest every year. This is the sort of obvious contradiction that makes all the talk about "complex systems" among cyberlibertarians seem patently absurd. In fact, it disguises a host of one-note thinking about the munificent and autonomous impact of technology, the relationship between politics and economics, and the methods by which power is held, controlled, and deployed.

But that's just it. Libertarianism is the perfect political philosophy for the high-tech industry. Once you've abstracted the world around you to a blipping series of ones and zeros on a screen the rest is easy. Ideas, emotions, passions, politics, history must all fit to the grid or cease to register. Libertarianism, with its one-to-one correspondence theory of political agency and action, is an entirely appropriate worldview for a world no longer seen as analog or organic, but digital, binary, and synthetic. There is freedom and there is oppression, and despite the fact that cyberlibertarians chatter endlessly about the "complex system" of the World Wide Web, the conflict is distinctly uncomplicated in their minds. Privacy, free markets, and the unfettered flow of information and capital make for freedom. Government, laws, and regulation make for oppression. On or off. One or zero.

Cyberlibertarianism's aggressive solipsism encourages and perpetuates exactly the sort of libidinal individualism that already runs amok in America. It also rationalizes retreat from political engagement. As it turns out, all the sound and fury about political freedom and liberty that overflows the chat rooms is most often about claiming the freedom to abdicate the actual complexity and contradictions of life lived in streets, offices, and factories. Cyberlibertarians fail to see this because they consistently indulge themselves in the fantasy that technology can resolve all the little messes of these supposedly outmoded ways of life. Forsaking the pedestrian social world in favor of digital bulletin boards or "virtual communities," single-minded libertarian drones—the true networked, cyborg souls of this brave new world—run rampant, indulging themselves with the fantasy that the one-to-one mind-meld they have with their monitor is a fitting model for social interaction at-large. "Computers," Borsook writes, "are so much more rule-based, controllable, fixable, and comprehensible than any human will ever be." Perhaps that's why a sense of community is so often found wanting in Silicon Valley. Borsook documents one particularly telling example of high tech's abdication of the real: In 1999 the United Way of Santa Clara County (Silicon Valley's true geographic coordinates) went broke. As if this weren't pathetic enough in one of the richest counties on the planet, almost nobody stepped in to help out. It took Bill Gates sweeping down from Redmond to prod the Microsoft-hating CEOs of the Valley into pitching in and bailing out the giant nonprofit.

gradually apparent catch being the godawful working hours.

Around the corner from our apartment a dot-com called Petopia moved in where a custom photo-printing shop used to be. Petopia had big glass windows so you could see the poor boys sitting at their monitors late at night. The "jobs" section on their Web site talked about the fun of bringing your dog to work. Well, at least they had a popcorn machine and a giant fire hydrant. Times change: The Petopia storefront is empty now, for lease, and the company's Web site indicates that it is now "part of the Petco family."

BARBARA EHRENREICH's *Fear of Falling* suggested ten years ago that corporate yuppies have given up middle-class professionals' traditional prerogative of doing useful, interesting work and are therefore more susceptible to the "addictive" attractions of wealth. A stock market derivatives programmer, for example, doesn't enjoy the satisfactions of, say, a professor or civil engineer. If you spend your days setting up the Wall Street equivalent of trifecta bets, you'll want to be well paid for it because money is your only reward.

Addictive is definitely the word, and—during the high tide of tech mania—the addiction had a twist: Dot-coms seemed to have improved on Eighties corporate culture by rewarding long hours with controlled injections of novelty and excitement as well as money—an appropriately Huxleyan approach for a place called SoMa.

To start with, there was the continual gambler's excitement of watching stock options shimmy on the Nasdaq. Then there were the silly perks. The popcorn machine, the keg in the kitchen, weekly soccer, the Informal Atmosphere. When Joel started one programming job, the owner took him out for Thai food and the new Star Trek flick. Another startup reportedly made itself an indoor beach with real sand. All of which was supposed to keep our video-gaming generation persuaded that even at work, Computers are Fun. If your leisure activities actually were your work, then why did you need free time?

The flip side of Work as Fun is Fun as Work: the creation of dot-com products by putting dams, flow meters, and advertising rates on things people do for free in their spare time. It turns out that if you do something on the

Net for its own sake, some third party will find a way to sell your enthusiasm.

My own virtual home is a Usenet discussion group where advertisements are either ignored or barbecued. So it was a shock to find that we served as unpaid "content providers" for Deja.com, RemarQ.com, and other ad-laden commercial sites that peddle Usenet posts to browsers and browsers' eyeballs to advertisers.

Worse, when the free services couldn't make a buck after all, they stranded Usenet contributors by cutting back. RemarQ dropped free browsing and posting. Google.com recently took over Deja's discussion archive, making it available again. That's good, but nothing says Google won't yank it off the Net when they discover they can't profit from it.

Another shock was finding that the commercial end of the Internet can't tell news "content" from publicity "content." In Spring 1999 I worked a temp assignment at a multimedia company. In the lobby was a display with the company's publications and a plaque bearing the advertisers' code of conduct. I reported to the "marketing manager" and she put me to work word-processing product reviews with no discernible sense of a conflict of interest. (It was not a hedonistic experience—the air smelled like hot photocopiers and I left with a whopping headache.)

At one point I applied to work for The Mining Co., since renamed About.com, which hires freelance writer/editors to manage specialty links sites on topics from Canadian real estate to Transgender Life. I didn't ask for the labor issues spot— too sharp an irony. The job was basically on straight commission, no promise of any particular wage. Payment according to popularity with viewers as measured in "hits."

They did find a labor freelancer after all. Eventually a nice Labor History links page appeared, courtesy of "a mild-mannered librarian in a quaint metropolitan library." After

Borsook is a perspicacious and frisky antagonist. She knows the cyber milieu well, and she feels at home there even though its politics make her cringe. She sympathizes with its hostility towards illegitimate bureaucracy, its impatience with nostalgia, its yearning for personal freedom. Not surprisingly, she has adopted the hyper, addled prose style and arch tone of so much online writing. She's fond of running multiple phrases and monikers together with slashes and dashes, as when she worries for the "non-high-end/non-best-of-class/but-maybe-with-quiet-virtues-of-its-own company." This is often cloying or distracting; it is a measure of how close to the machine Borsook really is.

In one sense, *Cyberselfish* is a casualty of the info-age speed-up Borsook wanted to capture with her hectic prose. Back in the mid-Nineties, when Borsook began to raise the alarm in various magazines and Web outlets, libertarianism was on the rise in the ether. But now, Internet anarchocapitalism seems little more than a quaint reminder of those heady, innocent days before the era of Time Warner AOL. Libertarianism has had its fifteen seconds of millennium face-time. The quirky, potty-mouthed rule-breakers of the information frontier got used. They lent their street cred to the corporate coup in hyperspace, and then they got fired. Little more than a stylish and well compensated advance guard, they secured an ideological beachhead for interests committed to the free market only insofar as it lets them freeze out competitors and capture niche-market monopolies. And that, of course, is exactly the point that Borsook dances around but finally misses. Smoke-screen it may be, but cyberlibertarian rhetoric has done its work. This humbug is not merely the Internet's "default political culture"—it is the Church Latin of global political economy.

Its vague sureties and fervent promises have come to shape the horizon of the possible on any number of "issues" from Social Security to environmental policy.

For me, the greatest satisfaction of working at *Wired* was the rare glimpse it afforded of richly deserved market discipline. In the days leading up to *Wired*'s failed IPO bid some wag had scrawled the only graffiti on the stall in the bathroom near my "work station." Half in jest, half in jittery anticipation he or she asked, "What are you going to do with your vested shares?" A couple of forgettable, smudgy replies were duly logged in the days leading up to the beginning of the end of this Web-dream. And then: nothing. Nobody added to the stall scrawlings, nobody bothered to have the graffiti painted over, washed out or sand-blasted away. Like an embarrassment that goes unacknowledged for fear of admitting the folly that brought it on, the question just hung there silently, unanswered for the duration of my stay on that sinking ship. The promise of financial liberation *Wired* encouraged its employees to expect has faded. The great digital revolution *Wired* hyped to the skies is no closer than before. In fact, HotWired was long a loss leader, and Condé Nast wouldn't sully their hands with such new media flotsam. Finally it was pawned off on Lycos—one of those Web site smorgasbord firms that are coming to dominate the market—but for all I know the bathroom query is there still, a monument to the folly and absurdity of cyberlibertarianism's unswerving belief in the benevolence of the market and a testament to the transparent fantasies that underwrite the way we live now.

accepting or canceling five profile-tracking "cookies," you could read about the Everett Massacre and the Pullman Strike alongside advertisements for *Headline News*, Shopping.About, and something called i-drive.com. It was an attractive site. Probably a labor of love. The guy's a hobbyist to himself, but he's a temp to About.com.

Joel found a programming job in a semi-academic research office and now can justify his shelf space. He's kind enough to justify mine as well for now. We feel less close to being moved out ourselves. At Joel's new job they gave him an employee benefits packet called "The Benefits of Belonging." Its contents included:

> Investing for Tomorrow's Retirement... Today!
> Your Group Insurance Plans
> Ensuring Your Doctor is a Good Fit to Your Needs

How nice. For us, that is. I hear they've ended free pharmacy service at General Hospital. Thanks to which a neighbor living on disability benefits has gone for months at a time without his seizure medication.

On those conditions, in these times, do we want to belong?

Driving home one night, Joel said quietly, "I never thought I would resent the computer industry." He learned programming in the early Eighties, as a nerdy hobby barely more serious than "Dungeons and Dragons."

Now some of us are watching cheerfully as the whole dot-com hallucination and its tin-eared libertarianism begin to fall apart. Maybe we can rebuild us a democracy out of what's left. Already there are signs this city is tired of being a boomtown. This winter we elected a pro-tenant majority to the Board of Supervisors, which promptly slapped a moratorium on loft development.

Still, Joel and I have talked about moving. Maybe the rest of America is no better than San Francisco, but at least in my New England hometown the policemen don't swagger on Harleys, and wealth isn't so openly defended against poverty.

I keep thinking about a nameless quiet rainy place with no millionaires, plentiful roofs and modest policemen. We could do with a change of scene.

TO THE MAGICAL MEMORY OF RAIN

Leon Forrest

OUT OF THE SUPERMARKET, on their way home with three bags full of groceries in their arms, foul weather struck down the day and swept up the loveliness in a monstrous rain. Felicity felt that she had been momentarily prevented from making any revelations to Desirée. They needed to hurry home. The street was quickly evacuated of all human life, except for an occasional speeding car, splashing rain everywhere. There was something terrible, awesome, and even magical about the way the weather had so suddenly turned on itself, Desirée reflected. She doubted whether they would make it home before they were consumed by the drenching downpour; *almost struck down dead* ran through her mind. Desirée suggested a cab. The mother said that they couldn't afford one, besides, it would be next to impossible to get a taxi to take them a mere four blocks. They could make it home if only she could get Desirée

moving. Well, this was what it meant to live under a tyranny, the young woman thought to herself. She was always using a mask of excuses.

Soon the two unfortunate women were the captives of a shocking thunderstorm, three long blocks from the street where they lived, lightning and furious rain pouring everywhere. Grocery bags were soon so rain-drenched that apples and oranges were falling upon the pavement and produce was flying about. Rain-sopped paper bags were falling apart and completely crumbling in their hands. Racing on their high heels, the women were a half block or less away from home when the heel of Desirée's left slipper cracked and the slipper came off. She didn't have time to retrieve it. Thanks to her years of ballet lessons, she was able to maintain a semblance of balance and didn't fall, but much of the produce came tumbling onto the street. Vegetables and packages of frozen meats were sucked up

Leon Forrest has published five novels, including the critically acclaimed *Divine Days*, an epic narrative of Chicago's South Side. "To the Magical Memory of Rain" is excerpted from *Meteor in the Madhouse*, the manuscript Forrest was perfecting right up until his untimely death in 1997. Forrest intended this novel, made up of five interconnected novellas, to culminate his life's work and the fictional world of Forrest County, which he had created in his earlier novels. It appears here by kind permission of Marianne Forrest. *Meteor in the Madhouse* is published by TriQuarterly Books/Northwestern University Press.

in the storm. Her mother was far ahead of her. And Desirée didn't have the time or the inclination to retrieve the slipper, but hobbled the twenty-five yards to the door of the old apartment building. Just then the paper bags were swept out of the hands of both women by the powerful grasp of the thunderstorm; as if struck by the wand of cruel magic, the women discovered themselves arriving home empty-handed.

As Desirée took a hurried, last look down the length of the street, she saw, approximately five feet from the doorway, the complete harvest of their two-week's grocery shopping transformed to litter, jetsam and flotsam, as it were, in the man-overboard mayhem spun by the windstorm. The brown paper bags whipped about like so much foolish garbage left over from a masquerade carnival scene; and Desirée's high-heeled silver slipper appeared to romp about in the rain. In the distance, an extremely tall figure, a dark stranger of a man, appeared, carrying aloft a huge umbrella, which miraculously enough seemed undisturbed by the wicked wand of the thunderstorm. The huge, lily-white umbrella appeared to have the power and size of a protective canopy above a freak side-show at the circus. As she dashed upstairs to get in out of the fierce storm, Desirée thought of the unfortunate incident as yet another example of the Dobbs's condemned condition, and why she must get away. Even the last sight, that of the tall figure in the distance with his huge umbrella, seemed yet another manifestation of the madness which now blew out of the rainstorm. A deranged set of circumstances which kept her and her mother on the brink of a living unreality ... forevermore. The mother regarded all their groceries lost to the thunderstorm, simply and bitterly, as plain bad luck. It was not unlike the reversal of fortunes in life, she wearily reflected.

Now Desirée was drying the mother off with a series of bath towels; then she gave her a fine cup of pea soup and put her to bed. No sooner had the mother's head collapsed upon the pillow than she fell fast asleep. Just as Desirée turned to the place where she had left off reading *Anna Karenina*, the doorbell rang three times. Shocked by the shrill peal of the bell, the frightened and bewildered Desirée crept to the door. And who could it be out of this terrible rainstorm? Someone beseeching them for shelter and comfort from some calamity, as driven as this terrible thunderstorm?

When Desirée opened the door (but at a safe crack, of course, as was her training—only to the width of the six-inch chain), there stood *the most absolutely gorgeous guy in captivity*, she heard her heart throb in her throat. He was magnificently attired, and he remained—astonishingly enough—untouched completely by even one drop of rain—not even the slightest hint of a trickle. *Well of course, he had the gigantic umbrella ... and oh my God is he forever and a day tall ... But,* the breathless Desirée exclaimed to herself, *just how had he bounded up the four flights of steps with such accelerated speed? On the wings of a dove? No. An eagle?* Now Desirée unfastened the chain, feeling completely safe in the lyrical lair of his hypnotic, dark, soul-draining eyes. Desirée had never heard her heart pump with such life before (except the times she had tried out for the track team, and had almost broken her neck—or so she had thought—attempting to vault hurdles at breakneck speed). ... It was like the rewinding of hundreds of feet of film, flashing backwards faster than any forward thrust she had ever encountered. ... *Oh it was ... he was too much.*

Just then the most gorgeous guy in the world said: "I've come for you, Desirée, to take you away from all of this," in a rich, deep tenor voice, full of mellifluous melody, honey, rhapsody, gentleness, urgency, and righteousness. *Just too marvelous for words*, Desirée heard her heart proclaim. At least that's what Desirée thought she had heard him say. Because he was just too gorgeous for words, words, words alone to know what exactly he didn't say; or did say.

If Vronsky looked like this, no wonder Anna lost her sense of reason, Desirée wept to her heart's delight. Just then the most gorgeous guy in captivity took three large military steps backwards in the hallway, *completely dominating all the space in time*, she thought. Then he brought forth, in the form of an offering, a huge white umbrella, which contained, *for heaven's sake*, the four bags of ... *no—it couldn't be* ... but four bags were set about in a perfect circle on the outskirts of the gigantic umbrella, filled to capacity and untouched by the furious rain. These items were in the same condition as when Desirée and her mother had left the store, she now discovered as she picked her way through each bag, going to and fro from the door to the kitchen with one bag at a time, as if to savor the miracle. In the kitchen she reexamined the contents with even greater thoroughness, finding her fingers moving over the contents of the bags, as a gifted harpist might touch upon the strings of her instrument while running through a sweeping, lilting version of *The Blue Danube*. Sure enough, all of the items that she and her mother had purchased were there (or, maddeningly, their equivalents).

Mistrusting her first impression, Desirée reexamined the bags filled with groceries—they were without wrinkle or blemish, though her face virtually wrinkled up looking at the wonder of it all. Her temple was rain-wet and soaked, as if she and her mother had never emerged from the thunderstorm at all. Then she recounted all of the fruit, for Desirée had a photographic memory of which she was quite proud, and didn't need to consult the grocery list the mother had written out. She said to herself, *I saw with my own eyes these very apples rolling down the street into the mud in the thunderstorm only minutes ago*, and shook with terror and awe. Desirée found herself trembling with an untold fire and throbbing delight and desire. She was propelled, like the track star she often dreamed of being, and she vaulted down the hall to capture the most gorgeous guy in the world, who had spun—out of some miraculous magic—

the life back into her shopping bag. "It is but a wonder … it is but a wonder … it is but a wonder," she howled over and over again, until she was back at the front door and facing her miracle worker with her face tilted back as far as possible to encounter the reality of the most gorgeous guy in the world.

When Desirée returned to the door, the most gorgeous guy in the world simply said, "I've come to take you away with me, but you must hurry, because we cannot afford to let this beautiful night escape from our grasp." He reached into a secret compartment within his jacket pocket—just beneath his heart—and the dazzling stranger said, "But how can you hurry along without this?" He then produced from his pocket the fine slipper that Desirée had lost, with the heel pounded securely into place. Now the slipper shone with a brightly polished glaze.

Captivated by the mere glance of the most gorgeous guy in the world (who was so magnificently attired in various phases of the color purple), Desirée was momentarily speechless before this presence. *I'll not put my complete heart under your hammer,* Desirée said to herself over and over again, in a self-fashioned litany. The material of his clothing appeared spun from silkworms. He wore a smoke-colored leather jacket. A fox's tail was drawn through each shoulder strap.

Finally Desirée found a portion of the power of her tongue: "Tell me … Tell me, just what is your name?"

"I have been called by the name of Reign," he answered.

Reign was tall and thin and regal in his handsomeness. His complexion was a lyrical blend of deep rich bronze, a meshing of many burnished browns. The vision of an immense chocolate bar filled Desirée's imagination. No blemish had ever dared visit his face, or so did the visage of the most gorgeous guy in the world appear to Desirée. No barber's razor had ever touched down upon such a face, she thought. The pronounced Indian-Caucasian features were pitched to beauty in his African-American, bronze burnished face. Just then Reign fell to his knees and placed the repaired slipper upon her unshod left foot— a perfect fit. She gave it back to Reign, ran barefooted back to the sewing room, and found the other high-heeled shoe. Once she had allowed Reign to help her put both shoes on, she discovered that she stood a full two inches beneath his armpits.

Now, in an attempt to help the girl find her tongue, the most gorgeous guy in the world opened his mouth and said: "You will need little clothing, either, other than that which you have on your back. Where we will be going, you'll be dressed and redressed to kill, from crown to sole. Notice how a rhinestone diamond has already been placed on the outer instep of your shoe."

Hearing her exhausted mother snoring away, Desirée asked, "But—but, what of my mother?"

"We are going on a great migration."

As Desirée appeared to ponder the meaning of his invitation, the most gorgeous guy in the world took off the handsome, brilliantly alive rhinestone belt he was wearing and gave it to her. He said: "Leave my champion belt of priceless value at the foot of your mother's bed, along with whatever note you feel you need to quiet her concerns. This is my gift not so much to you as to her. It was a relic of Ashante royalty in my family, from way back when. But now, hurry, Desirée, and sweep up whatever you need (we must not disturb your mummy's slumber) for our marvelous journey into space and time. I'm going to show you a world higher than any mountain, deeper than any valley."

"But you hardly know me ... And anyway, how exactly, Reign, did you know my name?"

"There is little that I don't know about the divine Desirée."

"*Oh*," she said. Desirée appeared now to try to outrace her heart, and fled to her mother's room with the unbelievable belt. *How will Reign keep his pants up without it?* she found herself whimsically musing; then, shocked over these stirrings, she blushed in her embarrassment. The deeply snoring Felicity remained undisturbed by her daughter's high-heeled footfall in her room. Nor did she awaken when her daughter placed the worshipful Reign's belt upon the foot of her bed; nor even when Desirée placed a kiss upon her mother's temple. With her eyebrow pencil, Desirée scrawled a quickly conceived note upon an envelope from the IRS. But the note contained no pertinent information, for Desirée could not say for certain exactly where she was not going. *Let me hurry for my binoculars to see this unknown world, and my camera to capture this unseen universe*, Desirée said to her pounding heart, which seemed to drum with the beat of the rain as it struck down upon the roof.

I'll not allow ... I'll not allow ... My heart to be under any man's hammer, Desirée said aloud, and almost completely out of breath now, as she affixed the straps of the binoculars, and then placed her gift

from her father into the camera case. Soon the most handsome couple the world has ever set eyes upon went downstairs, and onto the streets. Now Desirée—who considered herself tall for a woman—discovered that she barely reached the elbows of Reign. The rain had completely ceased, and there was a rainbow in the heavens. Desirée saw at the curbside a purple-colored stretch limousine, with smoky ultra-violet-colored windows. The most gorgeous guy in the world scooped Desirée up into his arms. She was completely breathless as they entered the limo. The chauffeur was dressed in black, and when he turned to greet his passengers, Desirée observed he was wearing a ski mask with only shocking blue eyes showing through; he had a red carnation in his lapel.

The limo took off in a cruising manner, *like a plane or a gigantic bird about to ascend the heavens*, Desirée thought. She had never been in an airplane in her life, she could only imagine that this was it, this zenith of overdrive. She had been in a limousine once before when Desirée and her mother had left her father's funeral in a car similar to this one, but not nearly as well appointed, Desirée now reflected. The driver of that limousine was also a part-time blues singer and steel guitarist—Lightning Chord Rodgers.

By pressing a small blue button on a panel, the most gorgeous guy in the world was able to present an extended, bright bar of worldly delights. A variety of liquors, candies, mints, miniatures of the best bourbons, scotches, vodkas … caviar … patés … More than anything Desirée was stunned by the wonderful glass mirror that reflected the beautiful image of this fabulous couple before her eyes: Reign and Desirée Dobbs. She wondered if he had a last name. Well, of course he did. But he was too gorgeous to need a last name. Still, "Reign" seemed something akin to a stage name a renowned entertainer might carry.

Soon the most gorgeous guy in the world took a small pouch out of his jacket pocket. He took out a beautiful oval shard of reflecting glass, with an oval-shaped golden border, and from the pouch Reign poured something that looked like snow, (*Oh, it isn't, silly girl*, Desirée laughed to herself) or confectionery of some sort. Now deploying a barber's razor that he plucked from the lapel of his smoke-colored jacket, Reign pressed a button on the handle and a glistening, six-inch blade shot out. Then the most gorgeous guy in the world commenced to segregate the fine powder before him into columns, and now, from a receptacle containing glistening gold-paper-wrapped straws, Reign selected one and proceeded to inhale several columns of the white powder before him through it. Turning on occasion to Desirée between inhalations, Reign exclaimed, in a beautiful whispered, throaty manner, that this experience was "more wondrous than the breath of an angel."

Upon another glance, after the breathless awe she felt when he looked into her eyes, Desirée looked at the two of them in the mirror before her, and thought she might explode with glee. For the mirror *now* revealed a man, this Reign, as the most gorgeous guy in the whole universe. Yet the power of the mirror's perfection, rendering up everything in such exact detail, suddenly afforded her another slant upon the eyes of Reign that she had not noticed before. There appeared just the slightest discoloration, as if a tiny dapply brush stroke had been touched up in the very corners of those divine eyes, reminding her of a doll's eyes that she had often touched up with Mercurochrome. *What a wild, crazy thought*, she laughed. He made an offering to Desirée upon a small tin plate of Russian caviar and a half glass of champagne. His face was still that of a prince, but since he had inhaled three columns of the white powder, Desirée noted how Reign looked cold, brilliant, not as sweet, yet perhaps even more enchanting and awesome than ever. In the mirror before them, this couple, thought Desirée, could surely take Hollywood by storm. Reign had uncommonly long eyelashes and Desirée could not tell, for the life of her, whether the eyes of Reign were velvet emerald, or velvet streaked with the color of purple. *Perfectly guileless*, she thought. Now the tiny flecks of red in the corners of his eyes had evaporated from her view.

As the limo floated down the Drive, her guide lifted a small portion of the white substance that looked like confectionery sugar, and she peered down into the pouch offered to her by the most gorgeous guy in the universe. With a wry smile, the most gorgeous guy in the universe agreed with this opinion, when she voiced it. And then he gave voice to his wildest dreams, by revealing to her the paradise that awaited her, as Desirée took part in the ritual initiated by the most gorgeous guy in the universe; and soon Desirée was in paradise as she followed in close imitation of his every word, inhaling the white powder through the golden straw.

Meantime up front, the driver spoke in a gruff voice through his ski mask, upon the car telephone, barking out orders to a series of command centers, or so it appeared to Desirée.

MOUNT CAPON COMES TO BOZO

A water wagon rides into town
  nobody from the waist down some
  body's moved to the Mirage Club

captivity underscores the strangeness
  of this life we'll believe like chickadees
  almost any seed and tanked up on Pike's

Magnolia Shriveler hung like a horse
  of a different color a capella pinto
  let the shits fall where they may

take Webster random in any one of
  every derivation yes Dad
  your son's an effete flaphead

and hedge hiccup emeritus
  I'm beginning to feel like Machiavelli
  edge the pond Archie

forget about that cockamamie Loch Lomond
  cocktails made of winces
  you have a nosegay for a heart

a mind scuttled by rum
  no echo chamber
  to sound surrender

—Michael Gizzi

But she did not dwell upon all of this for very long; because she was now enraptured in the arms of Reign.

B Y THE TIME they arrived at the high-rise apartment building on the other side of town, Desirée was breathless and seeing visions. Soon she was up in the arms of Reign as they came to the door (*like a bride*, she exclaimed to herself). They received an uneasy salute from the doorman. As they entered the lobby of the building, an aged parrot who was perched upon the five-foot-high ashtray stand leading to the elevator, started croaking:

Do an about face young fox …
you can't stand the paradox …

Soon the elevator was exploding upwards, but Desirée thought that she was about to fall down the quite visible air shaft (was this the *paradox* the aged parrot had referred to?), and she found herself screaming and weeping all at the same time, as she entered a vast apartment in the arms of the most gorgeous guy in the universe, and he closed the door. The lights were quite low. Soon the light was turned on full blast, and Desirée saw signs unseen by her eyes before.

All about the vast room Desirée was shocked to see young, languishing and lounging women naked or nearly nude. Some were in cages. In other cages she observed adorable baby lions. Soon Desirée was asleep. …

D ESIRÉE WAS AWAKENED by the sound of a prodigious crash, as if someone had broken a window with a two-ton wrecking ball from a crane. Just then, miraculously enough, the most gorgeous

guy in the universe was at her side—reassuring Desirée that all was in proper form. Then, in a matter-of-fact manner, he told the story of what had happened in the apartment just next door. Desirée was shaking her head in tune with the early morning airing out of the apartment, and wondering about her dream as Reign revealed what had gone down next door.

It was, simply put, the story of a man who had thrown a chair out of his fiancée's front-room window, after he discovered that she had been having an off-and-on affair with his brother during the times he was at work as a pilot for Eastern Airlines. After his explanation, Desirée's Adonis said that he had to "scurry off to work." He now replaced his silver-and-gold felt house slippers with his alligator shoes. There was to be a fashion show in this apartment's extension, starting at eight o'clock, Reign informed Desirée. It was now about six-fifteen.

All of the nude women were gone. Desirée had a splitting headache, completely different from anything she had felt before. She felt extremely depressed and all alone in the world; yet there was everything to keep her content. Soon she found herself longing for the fine white grains of confectionery that the most gorgeous guy in the universe had floated beneath her nose, at the hour when he had redeemed her, as he put it, from the street where she lived.

The next day the most gorgeous guy in the universe announced that he "must go out to work and capture the essences of this world." When he closed the door, leaving Desirée alone in the huge room, she thought to herself, *but I thought that*

Reign had said he was going to work yesterday. She believed she heard, just then, a strange noise in the hallway. Perhaps it was the man who had thrown the chair out of the window, returned now to hurl the young woman out of the window. Soon the sound disappeared.

Desirée passed most of the morning and afternoon trying on the grand stack of dresses and robes that she had selected at the fashion show the day before and that Reign had paid for by dint of a mysterious credit card that was pure white, like his huge umbrella. But she longed for his presence no less than she longed for the strange confection-looking substance he had given her to sniff the night before.

Desirée heard that eerie noise in the hallway again. Soon a key was twisting in the lock of the door with a sound akin to that of someone trying to get out, not in, it seemed to the frightened Desirée. Now the door opened, and in came this huge snake with his tongue licking about. He placed his head in her lap and declared, in a voice that was full of authority, rich and rather familiar: "Now you must search my head for lice." Desirée found many horrible things growing there, which also seemed to grow or expand, even as she killed them with a knitting needle. But amid the abominable field of lice and other insects, she soon found a steady supply of what looked like the confection-like substance the most gorgeous guy in the universe had given her the day before. She sniffed the substance, the snake left, and soon the most gorgeous guy in the universe returned.

He said to Desirée: "Were you afraid of me when I came in a little while ago?" And Desirée said, without particularly grasp-

ing the portent of his question: "No." Then Reign went about the business of his all-consuming work.

Now Desirée decided to go downstairs to call her mother in order to inform her that all was well. But in the elevator, on the way down, she encountered on the twenty-first, fourteenth, seventh, and first floors a vast snake. At each stop, these serpents entered just like a natural man. Desirée thought to herself that perhaps she needed some fresh air. Yet, as was the case when the snake entered her apartment and placed his head in her lap the day before, Desirée believed that nothing could harm her, as long as she was lodged in the apartment of the magical Reign— Reign, and the beautiful substance, so like snow or confectioner's sugar (that she blew up her nostrils with the golden-wrapped straw). And the ritual was repeated over and over again: each evening Desirée and the most gorgeous guy in the universe would sniff and snort "the white lady avenger against death," as Reign called this magical substance; then the snake would come in. Then the stranger

would return, who appeared now to re-semble, in the imagination of Desirée, Reign himself. It could not be, yet the tenor of the voice of the snake, and that of Reign, had a similar resonance within an echo chamber of sound and authority. It was almost as if they were working shifts, Desirée thought.

In the apartment, Reign wore only his silver-and-gold felt house slippers. In the streets, when he left the apartment, he wore one of his seven pairs of alligator shoes and a smoke-colored leather jacket. Desirée decided that she had to get out of this place. She could never get the most gorgeous Reign ever to speak about the meaning of the snake that always came in just after her prince went off. And to where—to work? Nor could she get Reign to talk about "the white lady avenger of death" that she found in the serpent's head amid the rank rot and the lice. And he would say nothing of the individual snakes that appeared at the four stops when the elevator carried her downstairs to get some air. Meantime, the wardrobe he purchased for Desirée grew more and more gorgeous: very masculine or ex-tremely dainty in fashion, by twists and turns. She had not until then thought of her dearest guide, her dead father. Perhaps with the power of his avenging arms, she could remove herself from this place. Desirée commanded herself, just now, to get out of this place. *Simon says, "Stand up,"* she laughed.

Finally, when she came to the front door of the apartment building, she en-countered the same doorman she had seen in the beginning when she first came into this building. The name *Reverend Elderberry* was embossed on the golden name plate affixed to his dark blue uni-form. Desirée told the doorman that she wanted to pick up a pizza. Then she started crying, and asked him to step aside. Then she confessed what was going on about the snakes she encountered in the eleva-tor, but said nothing against the most gorgeous guy in the universe, even as she did invoke the name of Reign. Desirée also said nothing of "the white lady avenger of death" in the snake's head, nor of the white powder she and Reign drew up through the golden straws each night.

But the kindly looking middle-aged gentleman Reverend Elderberry now said in a voice that sounded like an echo called up from a man twenty years his senior, "Young lady you are in deep, deep trouble. The man you are involved with is one of seven brothers; they are all magicians of various stripes. And most of their magic is evil, particularly your man, who has got you by the nose, as I can righteously see. *His heart is not included in his body!* He is one of seven who were born without a complete soul. Do you know what this all means, young lady?" His voice was full of urgency and dread.

Desirée discovered how much her body was trembling in the mirrorlike glint she gleaned off of the bold-faced purple-colored horn-rimmed glasses the door-man wore. But without a heart? And was this possible?

Then with a twinkle in his eye, the doorman's voice sounded off in a differ-ent way: "But there is hope in all of this. I mean, you can just split the scene, but that solves little or nothing. Look, highly de-sirable one, there is a collection of hearts in a great big bag under the bed, in the mas-ter bedroom, dripping with blood. Child, you must go get that bag and bring the contents down here. … And then we'll— you'll go from there. But you've been sucked up by the seventh son of a seventh son and number seven in this tribe of bad-men-trickster demons. … Go!"

Desirée trembled all the way upstairs, for she decided to walk rather than ride the elevator in order to give herself some time to think over what had happened to her and what she must now do. She climbed up to the twenty-eighth floor where she lived with Reign, for she also feared taking the elevator because the snakes might manifest on the twenty-first, fourteenth, or seventh floor. But born without a heart, nor even a soul? "Oh, my God," Desirée screamed, "How can he be soulless when he is so gorgeous and filled with heart? Has so touched my heart?" Desirée had already thought of herself as Narda, and of the most gorgeous guy in the universe as Mandrake. Yet the doorman Reverend Elderberry's words, coupled with the visitor snake and the emerging serpents on the elevator, and the white powder he gave her, which kept Desirée excited or vastly depressed. …

Finally, Desirée reached the twenty-eighth floor. Though completely exhausted, she entered the apartment quickly and immediately fled to the master bedroom to retrieve the sack of hearts. She went straight to the gigantic bed and looked beneath it and found the soggy, bloody bag inside a huge wash pan (which reminded Desirée of the kind of basin that the mother had often used to wash her feet in). Now Desirée peered into the bag and found seven actual hearts, pumping furiously on their own steam, or so it appeared. Amid her howls and screams,

she raced out of Reign's vast apartment with the blood-dripping bag in her left hand (*Oh my God, my father's binoculars and the gift of his camera!*, and so she raced back into the apartment to retrieve these properties, with her heart pounding like a drumming hammer). But it appeared as if her detour to retrieve her binoculars and camera was a mistake that would trip up her needed flight from this place of her captivity. For all of a sudden Desirée heard a voice so familiar, warm, thrilling, and sexy. "Stop! You think you can trip me up baby, but I've got front-page news for you." It was the voice of Reign himself. Then as she hurried to the stairwell to race out of his world, she thought, *If it is true that he has no heart in his body, then he'll not be able to race me down the stairs of twenty-eight flights.* Then in a voice she had not heard before, he said "I'm reclaiming your heart now." So, off they went and around and around did they spin, race, and swing down the stairwell. …

Desirée never knew that she could fly in a circle, in a whirlwind with such speed, even as Reign took long strides in those alligator shoes of his. But Desirée was so breathless from climbing up the steps that soon he was about to overtake her. (Ap-

parently the doorman Reverend Elderberry was wrong, she thought, about the most gorgeous guy in the universe, who had stolen her heart.) A ruse finally came to Desirée, and she swiftly dropped the huge, heart-shaped bag, three steps behind her, just as Reign—in seven long strides—would have overtaken her.

But because of the smoke-colored glasses which adorned the eyes of Reign, the most gorgeous guy in the universe had missed seeing the bag of bloody dripping hearts. It was just at this moment that the girl heard the voice of the doorman screaming to her to duck into the elevator (Desirée thought he had sent it up to her just in the nick of time), and as gorgeous Reign lunged for the body of Desirée, he tripped over the bag of hearts and went tumbling head over heels down the stairwell fourteen stories below, letting out a shriek like a pig being slaughtered. Reign landed on the concrete floor, face down—but no blood was spilt.

Meantime, Desirée continued to fly down the stairs at breakneck speed. When she actually got to the bottom step and onto the lobby floor, several people were crowding around Reign, and a doctor was down on both knees trying to examine him. Suddenly, the doctor's face turned ashen. The doorman Reverend Elderberry leaned over him and said: "You are wasting your time, Doc, looking for a heart."

Greatly irritated by this intruder, the physician said: "Get out of here, he is still breathing." But then he stammered a bit. "I can't seem to find his pulse … or his heart."

The young woman was heard now laughing hysterically, and none could hush her. "Somebody slap some sense into that bitch," said the serious and grim-faced young platinum-blond doctor, whose hair was now on end as if he had been hit by an electrical shock. Finally, after five minutes of her rollicking and bitter laughter (as if somebody had given Desirée a dose of laughing gas), the young lady was led away to an ambulance, while the doctor proclaimed that the most gorgeous guy in the universe was dead—for all eyes, if not ears, to behold. The doorman appeared to be shedding tears into a huge colored handkerchief. Soon the kindly Reverend Elderberry was fulfilling Desirée's request and flagging a Yellow Cab at the entryway to the apartment building.

"Such … such a wonderful man, that Reverend Elderberry," said Desirée to the cabby, feeling lucky to be alive.

"Smooth ole dude all right. But you should see his sons. They are a real treat and a trip, too," the bright-eyed cabby said.

"Sons?"

"Yeah. Right smart successful sons. Ladies' men so I hear tell. All seven of them."

THE POETRY OF COMMERCE

Minou Roufail

Not a great dealer, perhaps, since she had more of an ear than an eye, and not a classic art dealer, either, since she preferred selling to counting . . . but when the conditions were right, as they had been yesterday, when she could set the poetry of commerce in motion, as she had done, she could fucking sell some art.
—Dave Hickey, Stardumb

"WHO NEEDS GOD when you've got Capital?" mused art critic Peter Schjeldahl in a 1997 salute to Las Vegas. The saying might well have stood as art criticism's motto of the Nineties. After all, it's clearly the guiding sentiment of Schjeldahl's mentor, Dave Hickey, an art critic whose influential 1997 book, *Air Guitar,* is in its third printing and whose ideas pervade the little world of contemporary art. A self-styled renegade, Hickey has spent years proposing a vision of cultural renewal sparked by the forces of the free market, or, as he likes to call it, "democracy." That vision, in short, is this: The expansion of state-sponsored arts institutions in the Fifties, Sixties, and

Seventies ultimately led to the people's disenfranchisement and the rote manufacture of artists by a modern-day Academy. Both artist and art lover, alienated from the local communities that should rightly sustain them, are now hostage to the mandates of big government agencies. The commercial sector, however, promises liberation. Only unfettered entrepreneurs can create a vital art, and only paying customers can escape the predigested dispensations of the liberal state.

Like champions of the market everywhere, Hickey cloaks his hostility to the public sector in the rhetoric of democracy and freedom. But Hickey is no watchdog for Western civilization like Hilton Kramer or Allan Bloom. He distances himself from both cultural conservatives and the lefty intelligentsia, fancying himself instead a man of the people. A product of the Sixties (he even played guitar for Janis Joplin), he is a perennial hipster, outsider, and establishment-basher. His latest role is curator of SITE Santa Fe's Fourth International Biennial, opening in the summer of 2001. Along the way Hickey made a living as a gallery owner, a music critic, and an editor at *Art in America,* and his criticism is wide-ranging and eclectic.

Minou Roufail lives in Connecticut with the requisite husband, son, and dog.

THE MIRROR MYTH

JONATHAN ROSENBAUM

To refer to a producer's oeuvre
is, at least to me, as ignorant
as to refer to the oeuvre of a
stockbroker.
—David Mamet

There are a lot of complaints
these days about the declining
quality of movie fare, and the
worsening taste of the public is
typically asked to shoulder a good
part of the blame.

Other causes are cited as well.
When the old studio system
collapsed, the high-profile chiefs
who once put their distinctive
stamp on pictures were replaced
by accountants and corporate
executives with little flair,
imagination, or passion. The
exponential growth of video has
made home viewing more popular
than theatrical moviegoing, and the
notions of film as community
event, as theatrical experience, or
as "something special" have all
suffered terrible losses. More
simply and immediately, there's
the preference for loud explosions
and frenetic comic-book action
over drama and character,
escalating violence over
tenderness, torrents of profanity
over well-crafted dialogue.

But most of the blame falls on
the overall coarsening of the

Jonathan Rosenbaum is the
film critic for the Chicago Reader
and the author of Movie Wars (A
Cappella Books, 2000), from
which this excerpt is taken.

Air Guitar, a collection of Hickey's writings for Art issues, is dedicated to such unpretentious pleasures as basketball, cars, and the Gorgeous Ladies of Wrestling. The back flap tellingly sports a photograph of the youthful Hickey accompanied by the caption, "The author as art dealer, 1967." As it turns out, this youthful dip into the world of buying and selling is the key to Hickey's criticism: At the age of twenty-six, convinced that his professors were too ideologically hidebound to appreciate his ideas, Hickey quit graduate school at the University of Texas for the more honest, more all-American profession of gallery-owning. (His disdain for academia has only intensified since he took a job as, um, an academic at the University of Nevada at Las Vegas.) The story of how he came to reject the scholarly "priests of institutional virtue" to "make one's way in the world through wit and wile" is classic Hickey, one in which our hero defies the shit at the top and the shit at the bottom in favor of the democratic, "Emersonian" way. Hickey is his own ideal American.

It is Hickey's aesthetics, however, that made him famous, and the connection he draws between the experience of beauty and the power of the market that have made him such a characteristic figure of our age. *The Invisible Dragon*, a 1993 Hickey polemic that almost single-handedly inspired a revival of interest in beauty, fortuitously appeared in the same year that the Whitney Museum mounted its notorious "political" Biennial, a ham-handed effort to showcase identity politics that bombed spectacularly. Enter *The Invisible Dragon*, an attack on the art-world bureaucracy and its "administration of virtue." Although only sixty-four pages long, the book was enthusiastically embraced by an art world weary of pseudo-radicalism and self-righteous posturing. Hickey received the Frank Mather Jewett Award for Distinction in Art Criticism for 1994. His ideas on beauty started cropping up in exhibition catalogues, gallery statements, and the effusions of acolytes like Schjeldahl and *Los Angeles Times* art critic Christopher Knight. By the mid-Nineties, Hickey was the latest vogue in an art world he affected to despise. (He returned the favor by publishing, in 1999, a series of vignettes on art world types called *Stardumb*.)

Viewed in terms of the larger American rage for markets, though, Hickey seems less like an innovative thinker and more like the Fred Barnes of art criticism: In his universe, all things bad come from elite liberal institutions like government and museums; all things good emanate from ordinary people working through their trusted democratic medium, the free market. Hickey simply makes this familiar scheme palatable to the art world by steering clear of right-wing wackos and pretending to derive it instead from sophisticated thinkers like French philosopher Gilles Deleuze, whose politicized theory of sadomasochism Hickey uses to ground his views on aesthetic experience and, ultimately, liberty. In Hickey's spin on Deleuze, "Sadism is about nature and power. Masochism is about culture and, ironically, the law." The sadist is identified with the repressive agencies that enforce "'natural law'" and "'formal values,'" while the masochist "focuses on deferred sublimity and the vertiginous rhetoric of trust." While "'the sadist is in need of institutions,'" the masochist craves "contractual relations." Thus Hickey conceives of art as a contract between the beholder and the image, with beauty as its "signature." Art both gratifies the beholder aesthetically and instructs her in freedom of contract. Oo la la!

Hickey applies Deleuze's theory to the avant-garde's old whipping boy, the museum, while equating it helpfully with the state. The curatoriate may make overtures to alienated beauty—the "invisible dragon"—but these are farcical, for in Hickey's scheme of things the true artist and the ideal beholder can't transcend the imperatives of the institution. Addressing a hypothetical aspiring artist, Hickey advises that "when your movement hits the museum, abandon it. Your demure emblem now adorns the smooth state—resides in the domain of normative expression, its status greatly magnified and its rich social contextuality effectively sterilized." Hence the book's cover illustration, Ed Ruscha's rendering of the Los Angeles County Museum of Art on fire. Quirky, demotic organizations like the Liberace Museum in Las Vegas are, by contrast, said to be more authentic representatives of American expression.

For several years Hickey could be found dispensing this free-market philosophy of culture in his column in *Art issues*. Ostensibly "devoted to unfashionable enthusiasms, unlikely objects of desire, and other phenomena held in mysterious esteem by the author and citizens of his acquaintance," the column was even more powerfully devoted to the audience. According to conventional wisdom, most movies are targeted to the teen and preteen market; the decreased literacy of the filmgoing public rules out most subtitled movies; and there is an overall dumbing down of American movies, with a notable increase in anti-intellectualism. Many commentators are quick to add that as the public grows increasingly apathetic, apolitical, jaded, and cynical, movies designed for their delectation would naturally follow suit.

Let's concede that there's some measure of truth in all these assertions—as there is in most assertions, if one bothers to look for it. But focusing on the last statement for a moment, might not the industry commentators have their cause and effect reversed? Couldn't the movies, rather than their spectators, be spearheading as well as defining this decline? Don't they share at least part of the responsibility for this overall dumbing-down? Given the uncritical promotion of the major studio releases, one might even posit that the press, in order to justify its own priorities, maintains a vested interest in viewing the audience as brain-dead. After all, if it showered most of its free publicity on more thoughtful and interesting movies it would run the risk of being branded elitist. How much easier it becomes to wallow in the slime if you and your editor or producer are persuaded that it's the audience's natural habitat—that the audience, not the press working in collaboration with the studios' massive publicity departments, calls all the shots.

Furthermore, or so the producers tell us, the highly sophisticated forms of market research and testing that shape major releases at every stage in their development, from initial treatments to previews to final ads, scientifically prove that the studios are correct in their low estimation of the public taste. This is clearly the surest indication of what the audience actually wants, so how can the producers be faulted for catering to their preferences?

I believe that this line of reasoning is even more stupid, self-serving, and self-deluded than the movies it seeks to excuse, deriving from a set of interlocking rationalizations accepted by everyone from studio heads to reviewers. What's more, it's a logic that doesn't even work: The majority of movies made according to these "scientific" principles bomb. In fact, it wouldn't even be worth considering if it wasn't one of the central explanations for why Hollywood makes so many bad movies.

For a bracing rejoinder to this set of assumptions, try the following on for size:

"It seems legitimate to wonder how men of the perspicacity which has distinguished some of the best work in market research could have failed to realize from the beginning that most of their research practices were not adaptable to the cultural field. The very attempt to adapt them to that field was virtually certain to cause damage.

"Obviously, the premise of a stable audience with reasonably permanent and objectively verifiable needs simply does not hold in the cultural field. Transplanted from economics, this premise becomes an obvious interference with the free play of human intelligence. To say that men would always need warm clothing in cold weather obviously was a statement of fact; but to say that men would always need soap operas in America was just as obviously a plain insult. Yet the pollsters, straightfaced and singleminded, proceeded to ram their hypothesis down the public's throat; the public, unaware of what was happening, had barely time to gag.

"What was this hypothesis and how did it affect the public's

programmatic identification of Hickey's tastes with all that is righteous and democratic. But Hickey's love affair with the people is ambivalent at best. Indeed, the tuned-in "citizens" with their "unfashionable enthusiasms" are the only ones for whom Hickey has any real sympathy. These people are members of local, intimate communities like the ones that Hickey grew up in, where culture is ordinary, and where "participants" consciously gravitate toward good art—essentially, Norman Rockwell meets Andy Warhol. The rest of us—that is, the majority—are but fodder for the sadism of the institution, and Hickey pretty much can't stand us.

"Romancing the Looky-Loos," an essay dedicated to the pensées of Hickey and country music star Waylon Jennings on the burdens of the true and authentic sensibility, is typical of Hickey's preoccupation with these cultural constituencies. Jennings reminisces about the good old days when he played "for people who come from where you come from," likeminded people who "understand what you're doing, so you feel like you're doing it for them." But things have changed:

> "Right now, hoss," he says, "it's completely out of my hands. I'm looking at those people out there, but I don't know what I'm seeing. And they're watching me, too. But they don't know what they're looking at. My best guess is that they'll keep on loving me till they start hating me, or their Waylon duds wear out. Because they already hate me a little, just because I'm me and they're them. That's why they always go on about how *talented* you are. Because they hate you. Because if *they* had this talent, they would be you. The fact that you've worked like a dog, lived like a horse thief, and broke your mama's heart to do whatever you do, that don't mean diddly-squat. To them, it's *talent*. Supposedly, you got it, and, supposedly, they don't. So eventually you're bound to disappoint them."

Looky-loos are, of course, philistines, enviously looking in from the outside. They are fickle, insensitive clods who will never really understand you. Jennings's brooding self-image—"worked like a dog, lived like a horse thief, and broke your mama's heart"—invokes the heroic artist who suffers for his art (and all for the sake of "them"). Indeed, in Hickey's story, he and Jennings are literally going down that lonesome highway, "sitting in the shotgun seats at the front of his bus, slouched down with our heels up on the chrome rail, watching the oncoming highway between the toes of our boots." Either you lived like a horse thief, etc., or you're one of *those people*, who as Hickey says, "did not live the life—people with no real passion for what was going on."

Hickey's association of "real passion" with freedom-loving capitalists and of philistinism with the liberal state is a staple of his writings. "Pontormo's Rainbow," for instance, recounts an early encounter with an authoritarian sociologist he sourly dubs June Cleaver, who grills him in the school cafeteria for the purposes of a national study on the deleterious effects of cartoons on children. The moral is supposed to be obvious: Invasive, puritanical bleeding-hearts want to deny the TV-watching boy Hickey the glorious pleasures of being "ravished by color." Then there's Professor Walthar Volbach, a refugee from Nazi Germany who taught Hickey that "the government" and "the universities" only sponsor "Aryan muscle-boy" art—that is, "official art"—as opposed to the commercial sector, which was "a *Jew* thing, a queer thing, and a silly woman thing," a place where truly vital and truly diverse culture can flourish. So Hickey rejects his birthright as an Aryan muscle-boy to become a "soldier of desire doing a little business in the night"—that is, an art dealer. For Hickey, as for many American libertarians, fascism and liberalism are indistinguishable because both promote the power of the state. Advancing from this brilliant insight, Hickey proceeds to liken various art figures to Nazis. In *The Invisible Dragon*, Hickey actually compares the Museum of Modern Art's founding director, Alfred Barr, with Joseph Goebbels.

Hickey's response to the triumph of the "looky-loos" and their big nanny government is not to withhold his genius from the masses, like the best and the brightest in Ayn Rand's *Atlas Shrugged*, but to retreat to Las Vegas, a city that he imagines somehow to embody democracy itself. For Hickey, art is "a betting sport," and gambling is a metaphor both for the free market and the free individual. Hence he is able to argue that Las Vegas possesses both the "only indigenous visual culture on the North American continent" (you know, the neon thing) and freedom from class stratification. Since the city's culture is a product of the market's response to "private desire," it is unmediated by the state-sponsored custodians of fine art. In Las Vegas, he writes, "there are only two rules: (1) Post the odds, and (2) Treat everybody the same. Just as one might in a democracy (What a concept!)"

This is, of course, preposterous. From the hard-fought

mental health? Adapted from mercantile economics to a field where mercantilism does not apply, the theory assumed a shallow, slothful, and unchangeable crowd, forever doomed to frustration and thus forever dependent on the wish fulfillment of certain minimum needs—sex, glamour, adventure, wealth, power, and the rest of them. The whole range of subtleties which make up the pattern of civilized behavior was not only rejected as being beyond the grasp of the audience—it was dismissed as irrelevant to their real desires."

Ernest Borneman's commonsense dismissal of the basic assumptions of the American film industry in "The Public Opinion Myth" appeared in *Harper's Magazine* in July 1947. But give or take a couple of sexist coinages that were standard for that period, I don't see how it could be improved much today. Whether it can be absorbed and heeded is of course another matter.

Why it's unlikely to be heeded is a matter of simple economics: Even by 1947, the industry founded on the public opinion myth was already too vast and too solidly in place to contemplate the prospect of dismantling it.

Now, I'm not really in a position to declare whether the audience is right or wrong about anything. Properly speaking, the audience is so many things, all of them overlapping and most of them scarcely known, that assigning it a label in advance effectively means ruling it out of discussion—which market research usually does.

I suspect that any studio publicist or production executive who read Borneman's article today would argue that movie market research was still in its infancy in 1947, that the nature of both the audience and the film industry has radically changed since then, and that even if Borneman's argument once had some validity it no longer applies to the contemporary realities of developing, making, testing, revising, publicizing, distributing, and exhibiting movies. Not only has the market research industry become more sophisticated, but the audience has undergone profound changes, temperamentally as well as demographically: It's more demanding about some things (such as the quality of special effects) and less demanding about others (such as plots that make sense); it's much younger; moreover, the video revolution has transformed everything having to do with movies. Today's markets are defined differently because people attend movies as special events rather than as an everyday activity, the older segments of the audience tend to stay at home, and so on.

All these things are certainly true, but I can't see how they alter the basic thrust of Borneman's charge. Then and now, the operations of the media-industrial complex have been predicated on certain highly questionable assumptions about the audience, and charting box office grosses to "prove" those assumptions is merely indulging in a self-serving form of circular reasoning. The bottom line is always the same: the audience is ultimately to blame for what it winds up seeing. We are told that this is the downside of democracy—we can't always expect to like what the mass public endorses—a sentiment that can only lead me to cite Borneman again:

"Does the whole process of audience testing . . . really qualify as a democratic process? Does it not resemble an election in which only one candidate has ever been introduced to the electorate? Have we ever been given a freely available standard of comparison between the pollsters' "control

Continued on page 92

union organizing drives to the penthouse suites of the high-rollers, Vegas is a city of profound and obvious class discrimination. And while Hickey has remarked on the "queasy dread" inspired in him by the state's "diffuse network of proprietary surveillance," he seems to have no problem with the nearly Orwellian surveillance technology used by the big Vegas casinos. Furthermore, as James Surowiecki has pointed out in *Slate*, the city is "a supply-sider's dream: no corporate income tax, no personal income tax, no local earnings tax, no inventory tax, no capital-stock tax, no franchise tax, no admissions tax, no inheritance tax, low property tax, and a right-to-work state. Difficult not to make money when you're the only game in town in a Third World city-state."

But at least Vegas is not Washington, D.C., the capital of "this nasty little Puritan republic," and while relaxing among his beloved neon Hickey is free to deliver his overheated libertarian attacks on the public sector. In Hickey's version of democracy, it's all quite simple and direct: Works of art are submitted to the public referendum of the free market without recourse to the state's artificial sanction. Meanwhile, the individual, practiced at negotiation and consensus through cultural relations, becomes a free participant in democracy. And Hickey himself cheers us on in our war with the liberal state while his books and articles are published by the Foundation for Advanced Critical Studies and his salary paid by the state of Nevada. It's hard to argue with Hickey's longing for a resurgent counterculture; indeed, genuine discontent with the art world of the Nineties is what paved the way for Hickey's conspicuous success. But rugged individualism is hardly a new alternative. In fact Hickey merely replaces the radical democratic vision of the left that has dominated art discourse since the Sixties with a radical democratic vision from the right. Nothing better describes the bankruptcy of this vision than his chosen city of Las Vegas, a place with no cultural commissars and no taxes, and where the majority of the people are losers.

THE TOYS ARE US

Matt Roth

IT'S NOT OFTEN in art that the medium is actually the message, or that form really determines content. But computer animation is shaping up as an exception. Early, hand-drawn cartoons bristled with furry creatures, bucolic scenery, fauns: the familiar Disney pastoral. Computer animators, on the other hand, have trouble with nature: Their mammals are creepy as hell (think *Stuart Little*); they can't capture a natural human gait; and as far as they've come with facial expressions, you can still see the servogears whirring underneath. Computer animation's strong suit is the mechanical, artificial world.

It's a fluke of technique that has a huge thematic impact. The highly successful Toy Story movies, co-produced by Disney and Pixar, plunge so unblinkingly into the social order of *things* that you wonder that children aren't traumatized by the experience. Parents are also in for a shock as they recognize in the society of degraded objects that populate the *Toy Story* films certain eerie parables about New Economy America.

This is a break with Disney fantasies of years past. When traditional Disney animators tackled a roomful of toys, for ex-

ample, the result was *Winnie the Pooh.* The action shifted outdoors to an imaginary forest where the plush animals, free of their stitches, had a natural setting in which to work through their Freudian hang-ups—or rather, as Bettelheim would have it, where Christopher Robin could master the forces of his psyche before venturing into adult society. In any event, it was a world far distant from the satanic mills that produce, and the mega-conglomerates that market, Tigger dolls.

The toys in *Toy Story*, on the other hand, are acutely aware that they are mass-produced and mass-consumed. They're alive, yet never break the illusion that they aren't. They think and feel, yet never allow their wishes to intrude upon those that use them. If Pooh and company are comically self-absorbed, the toys of *Toy Story* are almost tragically preoccupied with an overpowering social system.

Each of the *Toy Story* films portrays the struggle of the toys to more thoroughly accept their status as toys. In the first installment, they have to settle all qualms they might have about being objects. The setting is the bedroom of a boy named Andy. Though populated by ostensibly masculine dolls with stud names like

Matt Roth is a writer living in New York. His story, "Dreams Incorporated: Living the Delayed Life with Amway," appeared in BAFFLER Number Ten.

card" and its best alternative? If the difference between any two alternatives is so negligible as to defeat judgment, have we, the public, truly returned a valid opinion? And, finally, have the pollsters ever provided us with the aesthetic training which would have enabled us to make a reasonable decision?"

Let's translate these skeptical questions into a few practical applications pertaining to the Nineties. The December 17, 1993 *Wall Street Journal* carried a story headlined, "Film Flam Movie-Research Kingpin is Accused by Former Employees of Selling Manipulated Data." The story reported that about two dozen former employees of National Research Group Inc., which handled most Hollywood test marketing, stated that their data were sometimes doctored to conform to what their paying clients asked for. These former employees ranged "from hourly workers to senior officials" and mostly included people who had left the company voluntarily. All the examples given in the story (e.g., *L.A. Story, The Godfather Part III, Teen Wolf*) involved boosting a movie's score, but one could easily surmise that the reverse could have happened on occasion when the studio for one reason or other wanted a movie to fail—which actually happens more often than most moviegoers realize. Before dumping Peter Bogdanovich's *The Thing Called Love*, for instance—a film about country-western music hopefuls in Nashville, all of them played by nonmusicians such as River Phoenix, Samantha Mathis, and Sandra Bullock—Paramount test marketed it by showing it to country-western music fans, a move that seems about as logical as previewing *One Flew Over the Cuckoo's Nest* in a mental institution. This may not constitute "doctoring" test

Woody and Buzz, his room resembles nothing so much as a harem: The toys flop into compliant silence whenever Andy approaches, and behind the scenes they jockey for "play time," which establishes their rank. Sheriff Woody, the favorite, takes the exalted place on the master's bed. The movie's plot is high harem drama: Woody, faced with a glamorous new rival, Buzz Lightyear the Space Ranger, pushes the interloper out of a window in a jealous snit. The other toys, routinely counseled by Woody to accept neglect with grace, upbraid him. The rest of the movie is Woody's discovery, as he rescues Buzz, that he was a fool to resist technologically ordained threats to his status. Partnering with Buzz, he provides Andy with such great play time that everyone is happier.

Buzz, meanwhile, has the even more wrenching task of accepting that he is in fact a toy. At the outset, he believes he's an actual Space Ranger, able to fly and able to kill with his lasers. It's only when he sees a television commercial for himself that he realizes the awful truth—that he is a kept object whose only purpose is to pleasure powerful juveniles.

This sets the stage for *Toy Story 2*, where the toys not only have to embrace their status as objects but, more specifically, as commodities. Their status as property is now overtly marked—Andy's name is written in magic marker on the bottoms of their feet, rather vividly branding them as chattel. More to the point, transfers of ownership are also possible, sealed with a simple coat of paint that obscures the "Andy." What haunts the toys now isn't loss of status within the hierarchy of the toy room, but the prospect of being traded away.

The movie's first half-hour catalogues all the ways toys can be trucked, bartered, traded, and sold: retailed in vast quantities (by Al's Toy Barn, whose obnoxious TV commercials earn the toys' special loathing); culled for yard sales by fastidious moms (especially alarming to Mr. and Mrs. Potatohead, who desperately cling to each other); stolen by unscrupulous vintage toy enthusiasts (coincidentally, the aforementioned Al, into whose clutches Woody falls); and traded in the upscale collectors' market (Al plans to sell Woody, a 1950s collectible, to a toy museum in Japan).

Toy Story 2 doesn't pretend that a toy's life isn't fearful and insecure and humiliating. It simply sets out to prove that there's no alternative. In their adventures this time around, both Woody and Buzz—the former abducted to Al's apartment, the latter leading the other toys in a rescue mission—are granted visions of authentic selfhood, only to dismiss them as hollow fantasies.

Buzz's path leads him to the Toy Barn's Buzz Lightyear Aisle. There he jostles to life a Space Ranger as delusional as he was in the first *Toy Story*. Where Buzz clearly sees dizzying stacks of toys for sale, this other Buzz sees ranks of disciplined troops. Where our Buzz knows that Space Ranger gadgets are just for show, the toy store's Buzz thinks his lasers dangerous and his anti-gravity generator functional.

Buzz's double manages to live in a bubble of purposive labor and instrumental competence—though it is a running joke that he's actually a mentally shortsighted Mr. Magoo, the world serendipitously sustaining his delusions—while our Buzz is caught in what Susan Faludi has described as a "culture of display." In fact, to differentiate himself from his doppelganger, our Buzz proudly displays his "Andy" to the other toys. (They cheer.) To be marked as a commodity—and to be self-conscious about it—is as much a sign of belonging in the toy room as it is in postmodern America.

Woody, the symbol of Natural rather than Industrial Man, has a more complex reaction to his unalienated double. In Al's apartment, he discovers something like a native culture. There are the other members of the Woody's Roundup collection: the Old Prospector, an oracular elder never removed from the box; Jessie the Yodelin' Cowgirl, Woody's sidekick; and Bullet, Woody's horse. There is gulch scenery and a miniature saloon. And there is "Woody's Roundup," a

results in the usual sense, but it certainly sounds a lot like predetermining the outcome.

As a result of this *Wall Street Journal* story, National Research Company, Inc. lost most or all of its Hollywood clients, and I've been told that its successors have proceeded more cautiously. One might think that such a revelation would cast doubts among reviewers and other industry commentators on an already highly dubious practice, but no such reflection or soul-searching ever took place. The industry needs its self-fulfilling prophecies too badly to tolerate skeptics and most film reviewers are hardly independent of either studio interests or their alibis.

Writer-director James L. Brooks, who received most of his training in TV sitcoms, is a talented filmmaker who believes so religiously in test marketing that he seems fully willing to compromise his own work to the point of unintelligibility in order to conform to its supposedly exacting standards. This curious devotion to market research was demonstrated most cripplingly in the fate of his 1993 musical about contemporary Hollywood filmmaking, appropriately titled *I'll Do Anything*. The movie was eventually released in 1994 as a nonmusical after a series of test screenings gradually persuaded Brooks to remove all of the film's musical numbers. As a *reductio ad absurdum* of the perils of test marketing, *I'll Do Anything* should be seen by everyone in its musical *and* nonmusical versions, but of course it won't be, because seeing how much better it was before all the meddling took place exposes the patent absurdity of the process.

So I'm afraid you'll have to take my word for it: Having had the opportunity to see *I'll Do Anything* as a musical, I can report that it was immeasurably better in that form—eccentric and adventurous, to be sure, but also dramatically and emotionally coherent. The fact that the movie bombed at the box office as a nonmusical doesn't of course mean that it would have scored commercially in its original form, but considering that it had an artistic logic and integrity, surely it had a chance of finding an audience if the studio had known how to market it. (Ironically, part of the movie's plot is directly concerned with test marketing.) By the same token, it seems impossible to imagine how the release version could have found an audience under any circumstances because its emotional and dramatic raison d'être had been removed; following the biblical injunction, "And if thy right eye offend thee, pluck it out," Brooks wound up eliminating so much of his original conception that what remained was meaningless.

If test marketing was used exclusively to determine how certain pictures could best be marketed and advertised, I would be inclined to consider it defensible on those grounds; clearly studios have to determine what segments of the audience a movie is most likely to appeal to, and to represent that movie in advertising according to their discoveries. In some cases, I might even defend the use of preview screenings to determine whether certain pictures could turn a profit and therefore whether they should be released. And I would agree that some directors, especially directors of comedy, can benefit from previewing their rough cuts to see when and how they get laughs before making their final cuts.

But using test marketing to impose last-minute changes on movies seems much harder to justify, especially because it assumes that an audience is qualified to make decisions of this kind. Of course we wouldn't dream of policing the writing of novels or the composing of symphonies in this fashion. And if knowledge and expertise are necessary to arrive at intelligent decisions, it's hard to

TV puppet show that gives Woody a grainy, ethnographic glimpse of his culture when it was still intact, where "Woody," the puppet original, protects the old and female, dominates his horse, speaks the language of the animals, and accompanies himself on his own guitar.

But Woody sees all this only from the outside. He recognizes the wealth of kitsch artifacts—from yo-yos to toy banks—as part of a marketing juggernaut from years gone by, his musical heritage as a collection of novelty records. Even his companions, backstage, display a distinctly postmodern consciousness: The grizzled, traditionalist Old Prospector is actually a sly Machiavellian whose dearest dream is to spend a comfortable immortality inside a glass case (a dream for which he actively sabotages Woody's attempts to return to Andy); and Jessie is a markedly lesbian Yodelin' Cowgirl, singing a tearful ballad, "When You Loved Me," to the memory of a girl owner who eventually forsook her for makeup. Woody learns, as all Third World people eventually must, that the past can exist only as a museum piece.

Woody's only real choice is between the mass gaze of Asians and the personal devotion of Andy. "When he plays with you," Woody gushes, "even though you're not moving, you feel alive, because that's how he sees you." The toys only feel fully alive when they're submitting to Andy's creepy fetishes, not when they're actually moving and talking. This is because Andy's virtuosic play life—each stray fifteen-minute session of which is a Cecil B. DeMille setpiece that encompasses not only the astronaut and the cowboy, but a cast of thousands of toy soldiers, potatoheads, slinky dogs, dinosaurs, Barbies (!) and Little Bo Peeps—is the motor of the political economy that the toys inhabit. A less energetic form of exploitation (by, say, museum goers filing past Woody) wouldn't be sufficient to support the ever-burgeoning population of playthings and Disney-licensed accessories.

This, the filmmakers tell us, is the only choice we have. In making it we have built an economy of self-abnegating customer service, religiously charged consumption, and sheer voraciousness capable of triumphing over the less orgiastic economies of the East. But the filmmakers also point to a looming crisis: that Andy will someday grow up. Adults in the *Toy Story* universe are rational accumulators. When they see a toy, they see dollar signs. But you can't run an economy that way. Without the use value provided by childish fantasy, the whole thing collapses.

The toys have no illusions about this, even though in the denouement—with Woody and Buzz safely returned to the toy room, and with Jessie and Bullet (happily "Andy'd") in tow—they act like any good domestics by sentimentalizing their young master's budding manhood. Woody claims that he "wouldn't miss it for the world," even though he knows that for him it spells the landfill. But these protestations come with a wink, as the toys turn their heads to Andy's younger sister ("Yee-HAW!" yodels Jessie the lesbian cowgirl). Andy may be on his way out, but younger generations will provide salvation.

That's the difference between the Edwardian society that provided the soil for *Winnie the Pooh* and the postmodern, New Economy America from which the *Toy Stories* have sprung. The older movie might have valued Christopher Robin's eventual adulthood, but in the newer film adulthood is beside the point. Like the chicken that's just an egg's way of making another egg, adults are merely the means for one infantile consumer to produce another.

defend the idea of spectators without these qualifications determining the shape and effect of theatrical features.

Test marketing assumes that an audience confronted with something new will arrive at a permanent verdict immediately after seeing it. But our experience of movies—apart from the most routine fare—seldom works that way. Our expectations play a considerable role in determining our first reactions, and once we get past them all sorts of delayed responses become possible; a day or a week or a month later, what initially made us querulous might win us over completely. The film industry factors out responses of this kind—responses that suggest we're capable of learning and growing—thus denying our capacity to change before we can catch our breaths. Determining that a film's success or failure has to register instantaneously, the studio then becomes locked into a treadmill of other assumptions that degrade the audience even further.

≈ ≈ ≈

AND THE TRUTH SHALL SET YOU FREELANCING

*H*elp me remember, God, that I can be reassigned, neutralized, or eliminated for a thousand different reasons at any moment. My leadership is precarious, hanging by the silver thread of the people's trust in me. Countless things over which I have no control can break that thread, including your call elsewhere, and I will be gone.

But they need a leader, and when I am gone they must have others to turn to, others whom they trust, who can tell them the truth. Show me those who can lead after me and better than me. Ruffle my spirit when they are near, quicken my heart when I feel their power, and open my eyes to the special effect they have on people.

Protect me from preserving my own position or power or perspectives at the expense of future leaders. When they point out where I have not led well, shut my mouth and open my heart. Help me make it safe for them to try new things. Let me touch the spirit of those who possess the heart of a servant. I want to know them and watch their energy flow into others around them. I want to claim them for this work and pray them into my place.

Oh, God of mercy, don't let me stay in this job one day too long. And don't let this all fall apart after I leave. I will not last forever, God. Where are my replacements?

—From "Succession," in *Leadership Prayers*, by Richard Kriegbaum

THE LITERARY VAUDEVILLE
Mike Newirth

Death Travels West, Watch Him Go

THESE ARE GROTESQUE times. When the visuals of daily life are punctuated by shaky images of screaming children; of the bloody bodies of Rogers Park Hassidim and of Pittsburgh's Indian grocers; of corpses posed in broken prayer circles and parking lots and libraries, it may help to remember that the lately stricken Ronald Wilson Reagan was a gun-owning man.

Recall him, now, ramrod tall against the die-cut Hollywood West, and forget for a moment the chalk outlines among which the rest of us live.

Reagan was a believer, a Life Member of the National Rifle Association back when such designations meant something. For while it's impossible to imagine the permanent gun culture without it, today's NRA is so bereft and so hungry for that good direct-mail cash that it has evolved all sorts of convertible-bed and Ginsu methods: shooting out thick info packs, desperate "threats to your rights!" mailings, and pre-approved "membership" cards. And lost among these appeals, among the NRA's "Get tough on crime! Enforce existing laws!" party line, are the origins of the current epidemic of violence. As recently as the early Nineties, the NRA was able to convince many that violent career criminals, pampered by soft-hearted liberal judges, justified unregulated arms for self-defense. But the population

of shooters we live among now—Harris & Klebold, Barton, Baumhammers, Smith—are essentially the NRA's own creation: Noncriminals steeped in the muck of mainstream revenge culture, they are the vicious product of thirty years of right-wing resentment. This shift from economic criminality to a cultural wellspring of rage—remember in this regard the scapegoating futility enunciated by Mark Barton, the murderous day-trader—can be tracked, like many elements of the contemporary rightist backlash, to the late Sixties.

If Sixgun Reagan seems anachronistic now, a frail addled senior beside the steroid-pumped, Glock-toting race killer, one must travel much further, to an age visible now only in ghostly tracings, to find how the NRA was formed. In *Under Fire* (Holt, 1993), Osha Davidson portrays the organization as a reflection of innocent American ingenuity underpinned by darker paranoias. Following post-Civil War riots in which the National Guard performed badly, the NRA was set up to improve public rifle skills. For several years, the tournaments held at the NRA's state-funded Long Island range attracted both international competitors and social swells. Following the abrupt withdrawal of state support, the organization collapsed in 1880, only to be revived in 1901, again through state monies, amid a bout of enthusiasm for "military preparedness" inspired by the Boer War. In 1903, the NRA urged Congress to create the

National Board for the Promotion of Rifle Practice, then secured a nice dispensation in which military rifles were made available at cost (later, gratis) to NRA members.

Membership swelled after World War II, and the organization's public priorities shifted to the "shooting sports," a telling euphemism for hunting. It was during this era that the NRA achieved its Shrineresque mainstream prosperity, a normalness best exemplified by the hard optimism of the steel-on-granite slogan emblazoned on its headquarters in Washington, D.C.: "FIREARMS SAFETY EDUCATION, MARKSMANSHIP TRAINING, SHOOTING FOR RECREATION." But some decades knock out all the props, and in 1968, when NRA Executive Vice-President Franklin Orth, testifying *in favor* of that year's Gun Control Act, said in reference to the banning of mail-order sales that

> We do not think any sane American, who calls himself an American, can object to placing in this bill the instrument which killed the president

he marked both the terminus of the NRA's mutability, and the death of the pro-gun moderation he espoused.

Over the next several years, an internal schism grew between older members, often war veterans, who hewed to the NRA's more traditional, more benign missions, and an alienated coterie of younger members who found a leader in the person of Harlon Carter—a bulky Texan in the Hestonian mode, a former head of the U.S. Border Patrol, a onetime commissioner of the Immigration and Naturalization Service, and an NRA member since age sixteen. Rallying a reactionary circle (including dozens of NRA employees fired in 1976), Carter seized control of the organization at its 1977 annual meeting. Known ever since as the "Cincinnati Revolt," the uprising retains the hot-spark resonance of Chicago '68 and the Boston busing riots: one of those moments at the thin edge of the wedge where a thousand angry Joe Doakses, fed up with the liberal bullshit, cracked skulls and took names. In Cincinnati Carter's clever band of Babbitts set the template for the NRA's ever-after unwavering stance on gun control of any kind, adding in that same year to the organization's charter an assertion of "the right of the individual of good repute to keep and bear arms as a common law and constitutional right." Yet, as Davidson reports,

Carter also possessed a darker qualification for his zeal, one he uncharacteristically obfuscated. In 1931, at age seventeen, he had been convicted of murdering a Mexican teen in a sort-of trespassing incident. The conviction was overturned on appeal; it seems the jury had been inadequately informed about self-defense. Carter later attempted to evade the tale, claiming it involved one Harlan Carter; documents then surfaced, including his original NRA card, confirming that Carter changed the spelling of his name two years after the shooting. Conceal the consequences of violence under comforting myths of home, hearth, defense: Carter's dubious self-justification would become the NRA's ideological stock in trade.

This is not to say that the NRA hadn't protested gun control laws in its various previous incarnations. On the contrary, an intensive letter-writing campaign it organized ensured that the 1934 National Firearms Act contained no handgun regulations, and focused instead upon "gangster" weapons like fully automatic guns and sawed-off shotguns. (Given that handgun market saturation was basically achieved in the 1960s, the NRA here scuttled perhaps the only opportunity for viable gun controls in the United States.) Generally speaking, however, before 1977 such actions were grass-roots and semi-organized, tangential to the NRA's larger priorities. Only under Carter's leadership

did a militant stance against any and all gun restrictions become the NRA's sole priority, such artful initiatives as the "Eddie Eagle" gun safety for kids program notwithstanding.

The NRA's shift was of a piece with the general culture of sourness that exploded in the Seventies. Mirroring the anti-government mood of the era's right-wing groups, Carter's NRA began to target the Bureau of Alcohol, Tobacco, and Firearms (ATF) for a series of petty, backbiting attacks; a few years later, President Reagan actually announced his determination to *dismantle* the ATF, fulfilling a little-noticed campaign promise to firearms interests. (According to Davidson, the plan was scuttled when the NRA realized that abolishing the feeble ATF would transfer firearms law enforcement to the Secret Service, a far greater menace to NRA dreams of manly independence.) Out in the larger culture, guns took their place in the topsy-turvy class war of the backlash. Witness the post- *Easy Rider/ Walking Tall* tendencies of backlash cinema, in which primal images of bodily violation and vengeance became ubiquitous features of populist morality. The genre found its apex in the "crime in the streets" films of the Seventies and Eighties, including *Ms. 45, Assault on Precinct 13, Vigilante, The Star Chamber,* and all the other bastard offspring of *Death Wish* and *Dirty Harry*: gory fantasies in which Bronson, Eastwood, and lesser lights like Joe Don Baker raised to archetype the figures of the rogue cop and the armed civilian, taking God's side as they greased sundry punks and humiliated liberals along the way. Unfortunately, backlash culture also left many grossly miseducated in firearms reality. To sample: Wallboard does not stop rounds, even when convenient, and if you fire your overpowered handgun an inch from your boy-buddy's nose (as in the kill-happy opener of 1994's *True Lies*), you will set his face on fire.

T HE TEMPLATES REMAIN, weirdly unchanged after twenty-five years. Decades after Hunter S. Thompson and his biker pals first stared down an enraged burgher's .357 Magnum, the quasi-libertarian firearms culture continues to speak in terms of a perverse class defiance that has now come to dominate even our coolest lowbrow and pseudo-lowbrow entertainments: From mall-rat hero Eminem to porno rockers Nashville Pussy, and from white trash almanac *Hustler* to white trash hipster Jim Goad, we can all, vicariously and up to our credit limits, put our hands on the Glock. Moreover, liberals' anti-gun hysteria serves only to stoke the NRA's increasingly isolationist bent. Here, as in other precincts of the culture wars, denunciation just makes the persecution fantasies of the extreme right more credible. This is why the NRA benefits so immensely from anti-gun statements in the mainstream media: Using its direct-mail connections, it is able to portray the organization, and every last God-fearing gun owner along with it, as rope-a-doped by the big combo of effeminate cultural elites and spineless politicians. Ultimately, every pious exposé of the gun culture's old-boy seaminess, in venues like the *New York Times*, merely rains fresh checks upon the NRA's bought-and-paid-for men like Tom DeLay, who nimbly attributed Columbine to the absence of the Ten Commandments only months after taking sage cover beneath his desk while his security guard took the hollowpoint of Capitol shooter Russell Weston. This is why "Today's NRA," despite the insensate pronouncements of Executive Vice-President Wayne LaPierre, continues to hold such valuable cultural real estate, the ombudsman by default for all American firearms owners.

More important than the cultural camouflage of gun rights are the precarious economics of the gun industry. NRA members may prefer to elide the darker possibilities of their "curious indulgence" in the bland language of hobbies and collecting rather than the red tones of mercenaries, armorers, and obsessives, but they are no more or less a market demographic than the underworld of crotchety libertarians, right-wing paranoids, conspiracists, separatists, and drug war foot soldiers whose consumerism ultimately underpins the "legitimate" firearms market. And heading off any simple, disinterested economic analysis of the firearms boondoggle is the NRA's greatest semantic bullseye. Turn away from the organization's endless Red-scare bombast for a moment in order to follow the money, however, and a curious narrative begins to emerge.

The shooting industry is the real power behind the American gun battle. Although the major surviving firms are either owned overseas (Smith & Wesson, Glock, Beretta, H&K), precariously solvent (famously Colt), or threatened by novel lawsuits, there is nonetheless a great deal of money in the distribution, sale, and resale of firearms. An unjustly overlooked book by journalist Tom Diaz, *Making A Killing: The Business of Guns in America* (New Press, 1999), seizes on this unorthodox approach in considering our over-armed populace. Diaz sidesteps the ideological foam of the gun debate, examining both the semantics of firearm fetishism and the way market forces (firearm manufacturing is an almost completely unregulated industry) have elevated what he terms the "spiral of lethality" over other concerns. He describes the curious legal patchwork that both exempts firearms exclusively from any consumer safety

of high-tech hollowpoint bullets, nicknamed "flying scalpels" and valued for their "knockdown"). The elusive corporate histories that Diaz digs up are equally chilling. Consider, for example, California's "Ring of Fire" companies, a family-owned group of small manufacturers that has flooded the market with low-grade pistols retailing for under $150; or Georgia's Sylvia & Wayne Daniel Enterprises, which marketed crude, easily converted knockoffs of the once obscure MAC-10 to both Miami gangs and the white-sheet market. Such so-called "ugly guns" bob like feces in the market, disdained by nearly all serious shooters for their low quality and inaccuracy, but they are the weapons of choice for spree killers like Giancarlo Ferri and Harris & Klebold. That's how capitalism works, and Diaz makes a case for understanding the gun industry, with its constant upgrading of bodily harm, as the prototype for the reflexive savagery of the market.

standards and that reduces to a vanishing point ATF oversight of firearms distribution. Diaz has a keen eye for the free-market absurdities of the industry, which suffers from cyclical downturns and saturated markets, due variously to the decline of hunting and the ironic fact that a well-made gun never "dies." More importantly, he explores how the increasingly dangerous hardware of recent years has dovetailed with certain rightist cultural tropes. Thus fears of rampant criminality in the Sixties fed price wars between makers of snubnose .38 "Saturday night specials," incidentally flooding the market with the ubiquitous concealable revolvers. Similarly, manufacturers harnessed Reagan-era survivalist paranoia to stoke sales of military-style semiautomatic rifles (so-called "assault weapons"); and after the 1989 Stockton schoolyard massacre gun distributors and the gun press pumped up fears of impending controls to spawn an overspeculated market for "grandfathered" weapons and cosmetically altered guns, including huge numbers of Chinese and Eastern bloc AK-47 clones. More disturbing to Diaz is the emergence of "pocket rockets," high-capacity shortened pistols that manufacturers have promoted in recent years without heed for the dangers posed by the proliferation of powerful concealable handguns (and

Even more unsettling, though, are the ways in which law enforcement feeds the gun industry's escalation of lethality. In the Nineties, as Diaz recounts, police departments nationwide began to fear a perceived "gun gap" between their own long-standard .38 revolvers and the armaments available to the "bad guys." And thanks in part to the fetishization of semiautomatics in *Scarface* and *Miami Vice,* there was some validity to this fear: Recall the 1986 Miami shootout in which two felons, armed with Magnum revolvers, a shotgun, and a .223 semiautomatic rifle, killed two FBI agents and wounded five even after being themselves wounded by 9 mm rounds. This had wide repercussions: Ignoring factors like agent unpreparedness, the FBI publicly denounced the 9 mm as insufficient for earnest firefights, and embarked on a sidearm review which, as Diaz documents, ushered into the civilian marketplace numerous new weapons in formerly obscure calibers. Law enforcement's rush to over-powered ammunition had the unintended consequences one might expect from such a mixing of lethality and bureaucracy. Diaz digs up enough obscure stories—like the nest-feathering that Glock provided certain New York officials in order to promote two unnecessary upgrades—to suggest that law enforcement agencies foster gun technology proliferation even if their rhetoric officially opposes it.

A more insidious effect, perhaps rooted in the fact that many officers are required to range-qualify only twice a year, is the increasing incidence of what police call "spray and pray," in which an officer squeezes off several rounds or the whole clip in response to real or perceived threats. It's strange how quickly multiple-wound police shootings have assumed the cultural weight that 'banger drive-bys had in the Eighties: poled TV lights and grim cops, enraged neighbors tragic in their shabby night-dress, a crystallized moment from a Richard Price novel.

One must finally pin all these darker trends in law enforcement—the upgraded lethality, the reliance on cut corners—upon our contemporary equivalent of Prohibition. What few victories we have achieved in our scorched-earth War on Drugs—and what constitutes a victory in a nation where booze and pills are God-given rights, where "winners" *do* use cocaine and where the chemical apprenticeship of college is every middle class youth's long-sought reward?—are dwarfed by the loss of public safety and the erosion of privacy. It is impossible to separate this war from the gun morass.

Manufacturers on every tier benefit, from the "Ring of Fire" .25s that are sized to teenage hands, to companies like Colt that have fitted law enforcement agencies with devices better suited to Omaha Beach in 1944. Meanwhile police tacticians increasingly elevate doctrines of force over all else: Dozens of our bleak postindustrial towns now field fully armored assault teams, carrying the ubiquitous $1200 Heckler & Koch MP5 submachine gun; a generation of young cops has come up with no compunction against using "no knock" warrants whenever possible; a

class of administrators has learned how to use asset forfeiture to acquire land and funds that frequently vanish within insular departments; and also, visible only on the margins, the millions we have profitably incarcerated. We witness all this, passively, and then must also watch as an übermenschen "tactical" team dithers for hours outside Columbine High, unsure of how to proceed, while inside a martyred teacher dies on a classroom floor. Comfortable with kicking in civilian doors, our cops throw themselves back on procedure when confronted with one-plus sociopaths armed with semiautomatics.

It is true that the recent spectacle of the burly federal agent aiming an MP5 past the famous little shaver's head while his pumped-up peers rampaged through the house, shoving and slamming, bodies fat with the arsenal of democracy, did cause some alarm. But the Elián Gonzales debacle was the wrapup to a public drama so scripted that Tommy Lee Jones should've been in there somewhere. During most "dynamic entries," of course, neither the set-chewing Mr. Jones nor the balm of television lights attend the forcible discoveries of grow-rooms or the precious, financially stabilizing powder. That the public sees nothing wrong with such "extreme" law enforcement—witness the already wearily accepted police tactic of using pepper or tear gas to torment protesters—ensures that the new playbook will become the norm, and that civil life will degrade into something approaching the TV-ready spectacle. Many

shall become acquainted with the battering ram's crash, with the tiny apartments filled with immigrants or blacks or working folk, with the glinting MP5s, fine German tools of perfect precision.

Even so, in this age of downsized civil liberties, one feels a perverse empathy for the foot soldiers, the urban cops, and for those who patrol an increasingly tattered, volatile exurbia. Unwilling to face the politicized darkness of their work, the enforcers face instead a combination of weapon-clogged environments, a spreading population of the "controlled"—the poor, immigrants, those with addictions or criminal records—and immediate public approbation, whether earned or otherwise, in the event of a "bad day." If some cops are racists or sadists, experience suggests a stout majority are not. But law enforcement by definition is dictated from above, and to get a glimpse of the future one

need only examine the "resurgent" New York, where it's an open NYPD secret that the statistical demands of Giuliani and Safir, as much as macho tac-squad culture, were behind the deaths of Amadou Diallo and Patrick Dorismond. Firepower is routinely chosen over less lethal options, from baton takedowns to beanbag guns, and if Dorismond's shooting occurred during the proverbial struggle, it was still instigated by the weird "pressure point" tactics of "Operation Condor," which evidently presumes that any African-American male under seventy sells marijuana in his spare time. One can only imagine an NYPD initiative in which hardened cops dressed as Rastafarians hit up Phish fans, rave kids, and Wall Street interns for Ecstasy and LSD, and nothing is what it seems.

Which facet of our contemporary gun violence is most intolerable? Is it the racist edge-city rages of Smith and Baumhammers? The cracked-up, nerded-out boy who opts for early revenge at his underfunded hell of a high school in Kentucky or Arkansas or Washington—states where guns are common as grain? The Michigan first-grader who gleaned from his ragged home the coding that compelled him to shoot a classmate in the head? The Baltimore or D.C. 'banger who pulls the trigger of his cheap 9 mm for reasons that can barely be understood within their tragic seconds? Or the "tragic miscalculation" of plainclothes officers who empty their high-capacity clips to put down a black man reaching for a wallet? Whichever, it's hard to deny that the national love of guns is wreathed in a bloodthirstiness that somehow negates the caution of millions of responsible gun owners; is choked with a quickening rage that, from the penny-ante fascism of spree killers to the "acceptable" casualties of the Drug War, is fast approaching conflagration. How long will the nation remain lost to this violent dream of itself? We may be haunted by the bland suburban familiarity of those grainy stills from Columbine, but the NRA and its industry backers will continue to ensure that the blood of the poor, unkempt, and tawdry will continue to flow in the street among the distinctive 9 mm shell casings. It is the grease in the gears of the gun machine.

I'D LIKE TO FORCE THE WORLD TO SING

The Making of a Yes Generation

Joshua Glenn

T HE THEORY STARTS like this: Plunged into despondency by the 1992 election, William Kristol, then chief of staff for Dan Quayle, fretted that the pot-smoking and draft-dodging Sixties were once again poised to disrupt the pleasant ersatz Fifties that he and his fellow reactionaries had cultivated so carefully over the Reagan-Bush years. Despairing that his generation of squares would never again see the inside of the White House—which, as Joe Eszterhas has now confirmed, would shortly be transformed by Clinton and Co. into a satellite office of *Rolling Stone*—Kristol turned his attention to America's youth, the demographic cohort that makes miracles possible. Unfortunately, as the theory goes, Kristol found little in the so-called "Generation X" to encourage him. As *Time* magazine had reported, these sullen young men and women were far too prickly and cynical even to vote, let alone vote Republican. Yet somehow Kristol had to convince these kids, schooled in the scorn of the Reagan-Bush era, to rebel *against rebellion itself.*

Or so, anyway, goes one of the more inventive conspiracy theories now making the rounds. The funny thing is how plausible it all seems once you start looking into it. In 1993 Kristol outlined a program for selling conservatism as rebellion in the pages of *Commentary* magazine, declaring absurdly that "now it is liberalism that constitutes the old order." At the time this seemed quite mad. Today it seems prescient. We all have heard about the clear-eyed youngsters of "Generation Y," with their faith in Wall Street and their uncanny entrepreneurial skills. Well, it's all William Kristol's doing. He has managed to persuade an entire generation with his weird logic. But how?

Two words, according to the theory: OK Soda.

O K WAS "DEVELOPED," as they say in the business, by Coca-Cola marketing chief Sergio Zyman, the same man who'd developed the "brainwater" Fruitopia, at around the time that Kristol was making his appeal to youthful iconoclasm in the pages of *Commentary*. In 1994, OK was introduced into nine strategically selected hotbeds of youth ferment, including Boston, Denver, Minneapolis/St. Paul, and of course Austin and Seattle; it was yanked from the market only a few months later. But wait, back up: *brainwater?* If you've always wondered about the inexplicable popularity of "smart drinks" in the early Nineties, wonder no longer. Remember: It was the CIA which, by experimenting on college students in an effort to develop mind-control drugs, inadvertently introduced LSD into the counterculture. In the Nineties, Kristol and his allies in the CIA simply found a way to perform the trick in reverse. In their impossible

Joshua Glenn is the editor of *Hermenaut*, a journal of philosophy and pop culture. He lives in Boston, Mass.

quest to conjure up a cadre of conservative youth who'd rebel against a Sixties they'd never known, Kristol and Co., the theory maintains, *conspired to dose Generation X with the concentrated essence of what they called "OK-ness."*

Hold on! you object. If OK was a plot funded by the conservative establishment, and carried out with the support of the CIA and Coca-Cola, then why did the thirst quencher fail? *But did OK really fail?* The transcript of a 1994 National Public Radio interview with Tom Pirko, the president of a food and beverage consulting firm who'd worked closely with Coca-Cola on OK, appears significant in light of what has since transpired. Pirko told host Noah Adams that OK tastes "a little bit like going to a fountain and mixing a little bit of Coke with a little root beer and Dr. Pepper and maybe throwing in some orange." When Adams expressed puzzlement that so vile a concoction was supposed to compete with such fruity stalwarts as Mountain Dew, Pirko boasted that "even though taste is always promoted as the key quality, the key ingredient of any brand, it really isn't. It falls way down in the hierarchy. The most important thing is advertising." ("The most important thing is advertising?" Adams asked incredulously. "No question," confirmed Pirko.) Coca-Cola's marketing consultant, laboring perhaps under the weight of guilt for his part in Kristol's conspiracy, was making a confession here: *OK was never intended to succeed as a soda.* The whole point of the project was to inject a hip conservative worldview, as expressed by the soda's advertising, into X'ers who'd been rendered deeply impressionable by whatever it was Kristol, et al. had put into the beverage. Once the message had been delivered, OK could vanish from the 7-Eleven as mysteriously as it had appeared in the first place.

Of what did that message consist? Recall for a moment the gloomy cloud that hung over Generation X in those days. Even the happiest organs of the mass media were admitting that X'ers were right to feel an oppressive sense of reduced opportunity, thanks to (take your pick) globalization and wage stagnation, an unchecked growth in corporate profit-taking, a glut of low-wage service jobs, pervasive undereducation, and the skyrocketing cost of college and home ownership. The young people were, as one *New Yorker* writer put it, "millenarian, depressed, cynical, frustrated, apathetic, hedonistic, and nihilistic."

Coca-Cola knew this litany well. According to a 1994 article in *Time*, the company had been studying the behavior and attitudes of teenagers for two years before it introduced OK—note the timing, again—through something they called the "Global Teenager Program," which employed graduate students from that hotbed of CIA recruitment, the Massachusetts Institute of Technology. Evidently concluding that global teenagers could best be programmed via deliberately downbeat marketing, the company proceeded to decorate OK cans with depressing art, most memorably a set of drawings of a

GENERATION BACKLASH

KEVIN MATTSON

It's back! Bet you thought all that blather about Generation X had ended, what with Douglas Coupland's sales declining and slacker movies failing at the box office. But, no, the idea of Generation X has returned with a vengeance. This time it's not about culture, it's about politics. Novelists might have given up on the idea, but political pundits haven't. They've discovered that talk about Generation X is just the thing for rolling back the welfare state. Having found a whole crop of young heroes to carry on the legacy of Ronald Reagan, they've convinced the nation that the motto of youth is Give us the market or give us death!

It all started back in 1992 (a year after Coupland published *Generation X*). Two bright-faced boys—Jonathan Cowan and Rob Nelson—had landed jobs in our nation's capital. One was an aide to a Democratic representative, the other worked for a direct-mail fundraising organization. As the story goes, they were disillusioned with life inside the Beltway. Sitting in a bar and pondering the sadness and anomie that was the lot of all young successful white people, they cooked up an idea for a

blank-looking young man staring dolefully ahead, walking dejectedly down an empty street, and sitting outside an idle factory with his face in his hands. In the Thirties, such images might have had revolutionary connotations; in the hands of the Kristol/Coke cabal, they meant something very different. This is why the *Time* article, having just described the unhappy plight of Coca-Cola's target market, continued with this telling remark: "At the same time, the OK theme attempts to play into *the sense of optimism* that this generation retains" (my emphasis). Dead industry and optimism? The inscrutable connection was made by Brian Lanahan, manager of—note the ominous department title—Special Projects for Coke's marketing division, who told *Time* that "what we're trying to show with those symbols is someone who is just being, and just being OK." Translation: They were trying to produce young fogeys ready to affirm—*to okay*—the existing order, to look up at those silent factories and say, "Whatever."

Enter the wily ad agency Wieden & Kennedy (Nike, Calvin Klein). Charged with the task of transmitting the message of OK-ness to a target audience that had been chemically prepped by the foul-tasting beverage, Wieden & Kennedy developed a marketing campaign that seemed to pander to people's worst fears about mass society; it featured references to indoctrination via television, tongue-in-cheek personality tests, and, centrally, an "OK Soda Manifesto." Copies of the manifesto are hard to come by today; I happen to have one that was printed on the back of an article I clipped from a June 1994 issue of the Minneapolis/St. Paul *City Pages*. I reproduce it here in full:

1) What's the point of OK? Well, what's the point of anything?
2) OK Soda emphatically rejects anything that is not OK, and fully supports anything that is.
3) The better you understand something, the more OK it turns out to be.
4) OK Soda says, "Don't be fooled into thinking there has to be a reason for everything."
5) OK Soda reveals the surprising truth about people and situations.
6) OK Soda does not subscribe to any religion, or endorse any political party, or do anything other than feel OK.
7) There is no real secret to feeling OK.
8) OK Soda may be the preferred drink of other people such as yourself.
9) Never overestimate the remarkable abilities of "OK" brand soda.
10) Please wake up every morning knowing that things are going to be OK.

In every particular, the "OK Soda Manifesto" exhibited those criteria that the psychologist Robert Jay Lifton identified in 1961 with the practice of "thought reform," or mind control. As in all mind-control cults, for example, the manifesto forbade OK drinkers from associating with outsiders, and restricted their vocabulary to what Lifton calls "thought-terminating clichés." They were told how to think and warned that the individual's own experiences could not be understood except via the group. The Reverend Jim Jones' Kool-Aid had nothing on this stuff. As a 1995 OK promotional sticker that came bound into an issue of *Might* magazine put it, "OK-ness is that small thing that holds everything else together."

Reading the "Manifesto" now one can see it as an obvious attempt to transform the then-legendary Gen-X disaffection into the watery contentment we associate with "Generation Y." OK-ness, as the manifesto described it, is a doctrine designed for those who grew up in the Seventies and Eighties wondering, "What's the point of anything?" The very things X'ers found most alienating and confusing about the world were, it told them, quite OK: "War," if you will, "is peace." Furthermore, the OK-ness of everything was something one could only "understand" when one stopped looking for "a reason for everything"; learned to distrust the "people and situations" one had formerly looked to for guidance; and, presumably, learned to trust the market. Sound too counterintuitive? Not to worry, the "Manifesto" assured its readers: "there is no real secret" to figuring all this out, so don't bother trying. Then the purposely vague formula for daily living: OK-ness was a movement, made up of "other people such as yourself," and joining that movement would bring "remarkable" results. All one had to do was to "wake up every morning knowing that things are going to be OK."

This may have seemed insipid, lame, just plain bad advertising, but it worked. Within months the media had spotted a "Generation Y" splitting off from the unhappy X cohort, a cheerful "yes" generation for a cheerful new age. "I'm not really into that rebel thing," proclaimed one zestful participant in a 1994 *New York* magazine profile of American youth. In report after report since then, journalists and analysts alike have agreed that Y'ers are much better-adjusted (read: much better employees and consumers) than gloomy X'ers ever were. "Doesn't Smell Like Teen Spirit," gloated the title of an article that ap-

national organization based around Generation X. Curiously (or maybe not so curiously) they decided that their generation's paramount concern was that evil old federal deficit. They gave the new group the spunky name "Lead or Leave" (LoL) and promulgated this ultimatum: Politicians had either to lower the deficit or incur the wrath of righteous youth. Despite its obvious silliness, the idea was a hit, and Cowan and Nelson quickly became media darlings, their visages splashed across the cover of *Newsweek*. At photo-ops, they appeared in the Gen-X costumes de rigeur—baseball caps pulled backward and stylish T-shirts. They even wrote a 1994 manifesto that they called *Revolution X*.

It read like a pep rally, going through all the expected motions. Cowan and Nelson began by rejecting the Gen-X slacker stereotype, then segued neatly into the classic we're-not-like-the-protesters-of-the-Sixties act: "No fire hoses, tear gas, police dogs, or riots. Let's face it: Most of us aren't looking for unnecessary confrontation." With great historical acumen, Cowan and Nelson argued that the 1960s—get this—*witnessed ideological partisanship*. But their fine, clear-eyed generation had said goodbye to all that; Generation X, in their words, was "post-partisan" and "pragmatic"—terms that would soon become fixtures in Gen-X political coinage.

Of course, when someone says they're not ideological, they're ideological. And once you slice through their rhetoric of noble neutralism, you find that Cowan and Nelson had a pretty clear, pretty partisan program. They weren't just sick of boomers and their silly riots, they were

sick of federal budget deficits and everything they made possible. Now, announcing that you're sick of big deficits might seem like common sense when the government is running the largest deficits in history, but Cowan and Nelson went much further than that, taking issue with the very basis of the welfare state. They couldn't help but frame their thinking in sobbing terms of the wallet: "Our generation pays the highest relative taxes of any age group in America. Yet we get the fewest direct benefits." Arguing that Social Security rang up a debt that would fall mainly on their generation, Cowan and Nelson equated it with the Vietnam War. Here was the perfect Generation X rallying cry—a mixture of generational anger with a call for privatization. Cowan and Nelson didn't just want to reverse the excesses of the Sixties; they wanted to confront the legacy of the New Deal itself, to rally their young troops against the geezers.

Lead or Leave left in 1995, folding amid bitter staff complaints, lack of membership, and mismanagement of funds. One journalist who followed LoL criticized Cowan and Nelson for "having half-baked crowd pleasing ideas and ... seducing a credulous press corps while leaving no substantive legacy." In fact the duo left quite a significant legacy, one whose bad ideas and self-righteous shrillness entrances policymakers to this day. LoL provided a formula for all future Generation X political groups: attack Social Security in the name of selfless, nonpartisan youth. During the mid-Nineties, organization after organization formed under the banner of youth and with this exact purpose in mind. There was the Project for a New Generation, the Generation X Coalition, the National Association of Twentysomethings, and X-PAC. Following the example of Lead or

peared a short time ago in *The Weekly Standard*, a magazine that William Kristol edits. "After a decade of Gen X'ers being despondent about their prospects for fulfillment," the story reported, "survey after survey shows teens exuberantly optimistic about their futures." In what can only be a giddy inside joke, it then proceeded to propose as the anthem of this young, GOP-friendly cohort Jewel's hit song "Hands," which begins with the line—listen to it yourself—"If I could tell the world just one thing/it would be/we're all OK."

It may sound fantastic, but think about it. Kristol wanted the Nineties to be an inverted Sixties, in which young men would wear their hair short, young women would wear push-up bras, they'd all scorn the Sixties and love swing dancing—and in which passionate young people would add the imprimatur of their youth to the conservative campaign to discredit those concepts, and dismantle those institutions, that obstruct the progress of the free market. All of which has come to pass.

Besides, what other than mental scrambling induced by adulterated soda pop can explain the brainless gang of generational "leaders" we are evidently now fated to serve under? Behold the fruits of concentrated OK-ness: 27-year-old ideologue Mark Gerson, author of *The Neoconservative Vision: From the Cold War to the Culture Wars* (1995) and editor of *The Essential Neoconservative Reader* (1996); 26-year-old economics writer Meredith Bagby, author of *Rational Exuberance: The Influence of Generation X on the New American Economy* (1998), and *We've Got Issues: The Get Real, No B.S., Guilt-Free Guide to What Really Matters* (2000); and 25-year-old "sexual counterrevolutionary" Wendy Shalit, author of *A Return to Modesty: Discovering the Lost Virtue* (1999). When OK was unleashed on young America, Shalit was 19, Bagby was 20, and Gerson 21. Each of them show the clear signs of repeated, heavy dosing.

As in the "OK Soda Manifesto," Bagby's *Rational Exuberance* began by drawing an unexplained connection between the disaffection of X'ers and the doctrine of OK-ness: "Enter Generation X. With caution—and on little cat feet—wary, worn before wear, fearful, and suspicious. Still, and in seeming contradiction, we came wrapped in the passions of newness and with the relentless energy that birth always spawns." Bagby may earn a tearful pat on the head for her maudlin "worn before wear" stuff, but she never did resolve the "seeming contradiction" of people being both fearful and optimistic at the same time. Instead, she rushed forward to define X'ers as good junior citizens, their little cat feet dutifully propelling them up the social ladder. They are "above all self-reliant and self-defining. We start our own businesses at a staggering rate. We take enormous business risks." For Bagby the proof of her generation's essential OK-ness was not "other-directed" goals such as world peace or social justice—although she does rant at length about Social Security "reform," by which she means privatization—but its desire to become millionaires. Her book described a string of successful young professionals whose self-satisfied photographs bore mute testimony to Bagby's assertion that "the 'X' in Generation X is the symbol for multiplication. For us the symbol strikes a chord because the most successful entrepreneurs don't win by adding dollars—they win by multiplying dollars."

Again and again Bagby's work betrays the telltale mental short-circuiting that is OK Soda's gift to American thought. Liking money, business, the market means you are a Republican, right? Nope. Bagby blithely insisted that she and her fellow brave new counter-counterculturalists were not only nonpartisan ("Neither Elephant Nor Donkey," as the title of a chapter in her book put it) but actually *post*partisan. "In 1991, when I was a college freshman," she gloated in *Rational Exuberance*, "the Evil Empire whimpered its last breath. The world changed. Our ideological battle [was] won." Everything was now to be OK forever and ever. All questions had been settled, she insisted, in one shoe-pounding soundbite after another: "We want a government that W-O-R-K-S—that delivers the mail on time, protects the environment, fosters business, secures our future by deficit control, makes our streets safe, and stays out of our way as much as possible while doing it." Bagby's latest book, *We've Got Issues*, offers an even more sweeping declaration of these non-principles: "Our generation is making it where it counts," she tells the world, "not in creed or controversy, but in shares and silicon—venture cap, options, start-ups, hedge funds, broadband, plug-ins, digital, IRAs, 401(κ)s—those

Leave, these organizations all went belly-up.

But one group, called Third Millennium (TM), did outlast the rest. Formed only a year after Lead or Leave, it had a largely indistinguishable program and self-infatuated style. TM also had a manifesto, which the group imagined as an updated Port Huron Statement. And TM founders were—you guessed it— "post-partisan" and (like all Gen-X'ers) hip to pop culture. In ringing language they declared: "Like Wile E. Coyote, waiting for a 20-ton Acme anvil to fall on his head, our generation labors in the expanding shadow of a monstrous national debt." The group had a single idea that it chanted like a mantra: privatize Social Security. As Richard Thau, executive director of TM, put it in a speech to the ever so nonpartisan Cato Institute: Social Security might seem like "social insurance" to the elderly (read: the has-beens), but for "my generation it is just another tax." And you know how we feel about taxes.

The big difference between Third Millennium and the more short-lived Gen-X shell games— excuse me, advocacy organizations—is that it has no qualms about taking money from its better-heeled allies in the war on Social Security. After all, just thinking about privatizing Social Security gives Wall Street CEOs hard-ons, and groups like TM are willing to help them get the goodies. So the corporations line up like dirty old men offering candy to little girls. TM has taken money from the J.M. Kaplan Fund (a foundation that has funded numerous initiatives to privatize Social Security), the Coalition for Change (whose members include the Business Roundtable and the U.S. Chamber of Commerce), Merrill Lynch, and others.

TM leaders have testified before Congress to call for the privatization

110

of Social Security and, more recently, Medicare. Sounds political, right? But no. As they explain in their own literature, TM "isn't liberal, moderate, or conservative, but post-partisan." Known for their assertion that more young people believe in UFOs than the solvency of Social Security (one of the most talked about factoids in the history of polling), TM has gone on to "discover" that 53 percent of young Americans believe that the TV show *General Hospital* will outlast Medicare. And polling, as we all know, is just as neutral and unbiased as a voting booth. TM simply lets the facts speak for themselves: If young people don't think the programs will last, well, gut them.

This is a formula that just won't die. It doesn't seem to matter that neither TM nor LoL had any grassroots following, or that their books and publications are but merdlets of cliché that no one reads. The money is there, the ambition of all those young successful white people just won't relent, and as a result new Gen-X "leaders" continue to shoot across the national firmament at a regular pace. The latest in this tired parade is one Michele Mitchell, author of *A New Kind of Party Animal: How the Young are Tearing Up the American Political Landscape.* Mitchell doesn't work for TM but she sure sounds like she does, repeating the "post-partisan" mantra and carefully honing the most important skill mastered by her Gen-X forebears: sloppy thinking.

Reading Mitchell's book is like listening to a child describe his or her day at school—story after story is thrown at you with few connections. Of course, her preliminary assertions are borrowed from Cowan and Nelson: Generation X "didn't buy into protesting as an effective tactic." Liberalism, too, gets trashed as the new, "post-partisan" generation steps into its rightful place. Mitchell announces that she associates

are our buzzwords." And a fine set of buzzwords they were indeed—especially for William Kristol's pals on Wall Street during that recent bout of national madness known as the Internet bubble. But beyond controversy? The cat does make one effort at leaping from the bag on its cute little feet when Bagby wonders at the book's conclusion "whether or not I stealthily interjected some of my own prejudices (oh, of course I did) or whether I remained nonpartisan and aboveboard throughout." Otherwise, though, Bagby is fairly consistent, insisting that free market capitalism somehow transcends politics, that she and her entire generation have been liberated from "ideology." A more accurate description of what has befallen her and countless other tidy young strivers, according to the theory, would be a kind of political hydrolysis, a chemical conversion to a politics that otherwise made no sense.

Another victim is Mark Gerson, author of the 1996 book *In the Classroom: Dispatches from an Inner-City School That Works.* Gerson, too, insisted on his nonpartisanship—*he just wanted things to work!* But while his book ostensibly recounts a year Gerson spent as a teacher at a Catholic school in Jersey City, the plot is just there to give Gerson an opportunity to mock bilingualism, diversity training, and the idea that standardized exams may be culturally biased. Gerson's most important contribution to the literature of young conservatism is an extended meditation on the central OK activity of sucking up to authority. He expresses shock at his inner-city students' marked failure to suck up to him. Tongue nowhere near his cheek, he recounts that he and his suburban schoolmates were accomplished bootlickers; that sucking up was the most valuable skill he learned in school. Indeed, Gerson even gives readers a taste of his ability, heaping on the praise for neoconservative mentors and heroes like Gertrude Himmelfarb ("one of the world's great social historians"); Norman Podhoretz ("a literary phenomenon"); Michael Novak ("one of the great economic philosophers of our era"); Daniel Patrick Moynihan ("perhaps the most gifted thinker to serve in public office in this century"); and Irving Kristol ("a brilliant writer of remarkable insight and great wit"). He describes a book by James Q. Wilson as "one of the best works of nonfiction in recent memory," and his Williams College professor and mentor Jeff Weintraub as "something of a cross between an oracle and an encyclopedia." As for William Kristol, the man who drugged and brainwashed him, Gerson describes him as "a key figure—some would say the key figure—in the transformation of the modern Republican Party [into] the party of intellectual imagination and ideological excitement."

When it comes to your conservative elders, apparently, "The better you understand something, the more OK it turns out to be."

Wendy Shalit, who went to Williams College with Gerson, is the younger sister of Ruth Shalit, the *New Republic* writer whose plagiarism helped discredit that magazine. Wendy became a conservative mascot in 1995 after launching a courageous journalistic crusade against co-ed bathrooms. "A Ladies' Room of One's Own," her call to arms in *Commentary*, was duly reprinted by that bastion of non-ideological OKness, *Reader's Digest*. She's even dated John Podhoretz, the straightforwardly conservative son of the professional ex-leftist Norman Podhoretz. Shalit's *Return to Modesty*—which proposes that anorexia, date rape, and all the other "woes besetting the modern young woman" are the natural "expressions of a society which has lost its respect for female modesty"—also identifies liberal feminists as the real enemies of womankind. "It is no accident that harassment, stalking, and rape all increased when we decided to let everything hang out," she writes. Shalit, who's been known to defend the Promise Keepers and religious modesty laws for women, has declared that "the patriarchy, in the form of a stable structure of traditional values, and the protective authority to enforce it, is precisely what women are missing, and desperately want restored."

Not only is it hip to be square nowadays, Shalit would have us understand, it's hip to be brainwashed. Describing her youthful conviction that feminists "exaggerate the difficulties of being a woman" in *Return to Modesty*, Shalit begs the reader not to "ask me how I was so sure of this, or what this had to do with any other part of my ideology. As anyone who has ever had an ideology knows, you do not ask; you just look for confirmation for a set of beliefs. That's what it means to have an ideology." In other words, "Don't be fooled into thinking there has to be a reason for everything."

What's So Bad About Feeling Good? asked the title of a 1968 musical comedy that tantalized Bill Kristol's generation with a plot in which nihilistic beatniks were straightened out by a happiness virus. Today, OK-addled young people have converted the frustrated idealism of Generation X into a passionate complacency. The patriarchy is neat-o, Shalit insists; Gerson gives the nod to the social and economic hierarchy; and Bagby puts the seal of youthful approval on free-market capitalism. It's like, get with the program already . . . OK?

liberalism "with crumbling housing projects, holier-than-thou attitudes, and 'wouldn't it be great if' theories." She tosses out the now-antiquated idea that class and economic inequality matter in any significant way. The *real* social divide is generational. It's not the wealthy who won't pay for public schools, it's the old folks. It's not the politicians who reject mentoring programs for prisoners (a strange but perennial favorite of the Gen-X "leadership" community), it's the old folks. Again, it sounds pretty partisan, doesn't it? Ah, but in a feat of great political daring, Mitchell declares she's *not part of the Christian Right*. She wants nothing to do with their effort to ban porn on the Internet.

Let the rich keep their money and enjoy themselves however they want: Once such a politics was known as "country club Republicanism," but to hear the Gen-X leaders tell it, it is a stance of great novelty and hope for the future. What's more, as Mitchell sees it, Generation X is, like herself, universally conservative on fiscal issues and moderate on social questions. We all want to repeal the welfare state, but, hey, hands off our Internet—which is essentially universal freedom (with a few commercial messages tossed in to liven things up) walking on earth.

Here's the new ideology to carry us through the twenty-first century: Roll back the welfare state, let the market take care of things, form a national organization, speak for those you've never spoken with, believe in the Internet, don't listen to liberals, flip off the elderly. Or as one of Mitchell's heroes brazenly puts it, "Either get it or get out of the way. We can work around you." Yes, Generation X has busted through and found itself. And what they've found looks a lot like unregulated, global capitalism. We've seen the future, and it's us.

TELL IT TO THE TEMP

Behind the Scenes at a Listening Corporation

Paul Maliszewski

To enter the company headquarters of Penn Traffic, the East Coast grocery chain, executives must cross a covered, glassed-in walkway. Down below, Penn Traffic's warehouse operation is in full swing. Semis back up to docking bays, forklifts pivot, turn, and speed away, and warehouse workers prepare pallets for stacking. While the executives and their white-collar subordinates— secretaries, accountants, computer types, and temporary clerical workers like me— take the elevated walkway across to the offices, blue-collar workers down below have a separate entrance around back, through high chain-link gates. So well-insulated are the executive offices that all one can ever hear from below is the rare muffled shout, the faint sound of something very heavy dropping, and that steady, vaguely ominous beep that trucks and forklifts make when going in reverse. Yet in the summer of 1996, the executives above were trying desperately to listen to the world down below. They did so in the only way they knew how: with a professionally conducted survey.

Penn Traffic was in trouble. "The long view over the last three years has not been a good one, quite frankly," company spokesman Marc Jampole put it at the time, in what passes for disarming forthrightness in PR circles. Quite frankly, Penn Traffic had one foot in the grave. The company's saga followed an all-too-familiar storyline: New York City investment firm with no experience in the grocery business orchestrates buy-out with junk bond financing. Strategies begin to look misguided once the debt starts creeping up and the effects of the champagne wear off. In 1995 the company posts losses of $79.6 million. In November of that year, it decides now might not be a good time to build new stores. In January 1996, some of the stores ask union employees to accept a 10 percent pay cut. The union accepts. In September of that year, Standard & Poor's lowers the company's credit rating, warning investors off. Shares in the company, which traded on the New York Stock Exchange for $45 in 1993, slide to and remain stuck in the low single-digits. All other indices of the company's welfare—cash flow, revenue, sales per square foot—seem locked in a tailspin.

At this exceedingly iffy moment in the company's history, executives at Penn Traffic decided it was a great time to find out what their workers were thinking about. They hired a consumer research company to survey their 27,000 employees. With so much going so sour at Penn Traffic and with the company's workers surely hearing and reading the bad news most every night, perhaps a survey seemed like the least expensive and most hassle-free method to appear concerned and communicate that eager, can-do, wrong-righting energy. Surely executives didn't actually believe that dim spirits and low morale lay at the heart of the company's woes. It wasn't the sackers and cashiers who accumulated all that debt.

It was also at this moment that the temp agency I'd been working for off and on, three days here, three days there, called me and told me to report to Penn Traffic's department of human resources to read the survey responses.

John Pierce, the director of human resources, showed me to a desk stacked high with paper and surrounded by boxes filled with more paper. Closed boxes lined the carpeted partitions of the cubicle and were wedged tightly underneath the desk, supporting it on one side. Were it not for the computer shoved into the corner, the cubicle might have been pre-Dickensian. The boxes stacked along the top bulged at the sides, the weight of their contents crushing the tops of the cartons below. Someone with a flair for the triple-digit font size had labeled the boxes with a magic marker. They read "Big Bear," "Quality," "Riverside," and "Insalaco," words and near-words which meant absolutely nothing to me then and which I wrongly took to be code names for some project or other.

These papers, Pierce told me, with a slight note of pride, comprised every single response to a single question of the professionally conducted survey. As he told me about the survey (very costly for the company, the results very important) and filled me in on the basics (half hour for lunch, come get me if you have any questions, or, better yet, ask my secretary), Pierce stepped over to one of the open boxes, reached in and pulled out bunches of the responses, rubber-banded together in groups of roughly a hundred. He riffled through the pages a couple of times and then quickly dropped them back into the box. A few of the surveys were already in a modest stack by the computer, the rubber band off, a sure sign that some temp, some other Bartleby preferring not to, was here before me and had quit or been fired in the middle of things.

The question that I was to spend the next six weeks pondering was Part B of the "Optional Comments Section" and what's known pedagogically as your free response type question: "What are your suggestions for the way employees should be recognized or rewarded for providing excellent service to customers?" Seems simple enough. The catch was that Pierce and Penn Traffic wanted the responses quantified. After I questioned Pierce about what he meant exactly by "quantified" and ascertained that he didn't, as I hoped, mean "summarize"—he wanted numbers only—I settled in among the pages and began to read the responses in earnest.

Some of the quantifying wasn't nearly as messy as I had originally feared. If an employee wrote "I want a raise for my excellent customer service," I would simply chalk another one up in the "raise" column of my ever-expanding spreadsheet. And each time I came across a response reading, "Money talks, bullshit

"I don't want
our people hurt!"

quires you to risk death just to go to a low-paying job then something here is pretty messed up!" I believe I counted this as a vote for making sure all merit programs are fair. But as soon as I resolved one dicey response, another turned up: "Our employee appreciation day consisted of two bags of Food Club pretzels, one bag of Food Club chips and five bottles of Insalaco's soda. It was thrown in the breakroom." Is that a yea for more soda? A nay for Food Club brand snacks? I added one hash mark to the "dinner/picnic" category and continued on. Common sense told me all the responses read like votes for better jobs, but that wasn't the question the survey was asking.

As I made my way through the pages, time after time I came across category-busting responses. There was a long narrative about the favoritism shown to the head meat cutter at Store 65, who supposedly whiles the hours away in the manager's office, leaving the respondent and others to pick up his slack and take customers for meat and seafood. I wished that I could somehow find the questionnaire from this head meat cutter at Store 65 and discard it, uncounted. But the only thing that counted was my counting, and my counting was flawed by the impossibility of quantifying frustration.

I couldn't do justice to the employees' sense that the survey was a futile waste of money—as many pointed out, hazarding guesses as to its cost—because nobody was asking about frustration. All Penn Traffic was interested in hearing about was the narrowly circumscribed matter of rewarding employees for excellent customer service. "Keep promoting, recognizing, and rewarding the suck asses," one

walks"—I cannot tell you how many times I read some version of that sentence—I felt I was honoring the letter of the response when I added another vote for the Party of the Raise. As for the spirit of nearly all the responses—that, regrettably, fell between the long columns of my spreadsheet.

But the surveys required judgment calls, and each nettlesome judgment call revealed some serious conceptual flaw with my spreadsheet. I had expanded it to nineteen hopelessly general categories—profit-sharing, bonus, extra break during the day, special parking space, scheduling consideration, personal letter, just say thanks, and so forth—and I knew there was plenty else that the employees had written that could never be expressed in numbers. How to count the respondent who wrote: "One day during the winter, we were having really bad weather and a few employees got merit awards for coming to work. If getting a merit award re-

employee wrote. "This includes the ones that sleep their way up." I slotted this response with others under "Any reward system needs to be fair." Another employee wrote, "In one department in our store we had two employees from a juvenile delinquency home, a recovering crack addict, and a thief." It was decided—with everything the passive voice implies—that the co-worker of the recovering addict counted under my most general category of all, store relations.

I was reading the complaints, word for word all of them, but they weren't going anywhere beyond me and the little scraps of paper onto which I transcribed what they'd written, scraps of paper that I folded in half and tucked into my shirt pocket every day before leaving. Barely an hour into my task, its absurdity was obvious: I was a $7.25-an-hour temp, reading and analyzing—excuse me, quantifying—the anger and frustration of people I didn't know, employed in a business I knew nothing about, for the benefit of managers determined to ignore the results.

When I ran out of paper to read, I totaled up my spreadsheet, tabulating both store-wide subtotals and company-wide totals, condensed my findings into a brisk, short-paragraphed, bullet-ridden, nine-page report and submitted it to Pierce. I sat at the edge of his desk, looking at the photographs of airplanes on the wall (Pierce was an amateur pilot) and waiting until he read what I wrote. I was somewhat nervous about how he'd receive my "Concluding Remarks" section:

I will end this report as many of the employees ended their responses. I hope you read what we wrote, they said. I hope you actually read these and something

comes of them. It's not necessary to read all the responses as I did. To learn what the employees are thinking, it's not even necessary to read all the responses from your particular store or your area of responsibility. But still a portion of these should be required reading, for everyone. Take a dozen or two dozen of the responses, pick them at random, and read them. The numbers and my report cannot adequately represent and do justice to the employees' emotions. Your employees are not simply mad or happy, unsatisfied or satisfied. They are not for a raise or for pins and pens. Many are frustrated, yes, but hopeful that they won't always be.

When he finished, he looked up at me, appearing immensely tired all of a sudden. "Now you know how things are here," he said. I agreed, not sure where he was going with this. Now I must kill you? He reminded me that I alone had read all the responses to the question on rewards for excellent customer service. I returned a vague platitude about how I couldn't pretend to understand the grocery business after reading these, but I thought I had a better appreciation for the work. For a long moment Pierce stared down at the report in front him. Then he flipped through the pages once more, looked up at me, and asked if there was any way at all I could make the report shorter. The executives who will get this are very busy,

he told me somewhat apologetically, then stressing that this report would fall on the desks of the company's highest officials. Pierce worried that he was liable to lose them after five pages. I told him I guessed I could single-space it.

II

A NUMBER OF MONTHS and a few other, less interesting temp jobs later, I read in April that Penn Traffic had hired a new CEO, one Phil Hawkins. As the Syracuse *Herald American* piquantly described it, Hawkins was charged with "creating a map to steer Penn Traffic out of its stormy financial waters." Like the previous regime, Hawkins put great emphasis on "listening." Listening to customers, listening to employees, listening to everyone and learning what they have to teach. He traveled to individual stores to meet with Penn Traffic's employees in what were billed as "Heart of the Matter" seminars, meetings that one reporter described as "emotion-drenched." In an interview with the Syracuse paper, Hawkins offered a peek at what went on at the Heart meetings. "We talk about a culture that we're trying to bring to the company," he said. "The culture is really one of managing from the heart." No longer would Penn Traffic be one of those top-down, dictatorial grocery chains. According to Hawkins, formerly demoralized employ-

ees were "empowered" by his seminars. Asked to explain something called "change exercises," a component of the Heart seminars, Hawkins elaborated at length:

> It's actually a little exercise where everybody in the room stands up, looks at each other, and the other person has to turn around and you have to change six things about yourself real quick and see how fast the other person can notice it. And once you go through the change, then you say, okay, now do you think you can live with that change? Or, take one of the more difficult changes that you did, do you think you can live with that change throughout the rest of the day?

I was probably more interested in Hawkins and his quest to build the grocery store with a human face and a great big heart than most people in Syracuse. In fact, I'll wager I was the only person outside of the Hawkins family who was clipping articles about him. I wanted to know what his new emphasis on listening would mean in light of what I'd read in the survey responses. Sure, I was skeptical of the Heart of the Matter seminars. No, I didn't want to experiment with any change exercises on myself. Still, hadn't I recommended much the same course in my report, perhaps without all that truly execrable Personal Empowerment language? Maybe I wouldn't have phrased things just the way Hawkins did, but still I wanted to give Hawkins the benefit of the doubt. Until I saw his ads.

The ads were abbreviated Heart seminars set to uplifting music and carried along on gritty, verité camerawork. Hawkins held forth among the gathered. He worked the room like a Tony Robbins without all the distracting glow and gleam, and his speeches blended equal parts corporate pep talk, promises of a better tomorrow, New Age bromides, and good old-fashioned ass-chewing. He was a marked contrast to Roy Flood, one of the managers he replaced. Flood wore a full suit in ads and only rarely appeared in the frame with workers. Standing among the bounty of modern agribusiness's year-round growing season and tossing an apple into the air, Flood looked as if he hadn't handled produce before. Where Flood was old, not what you'd call trim, and balding, Hawkins was new and improved—younger, trim, and less balding. With his tie loosened and his coat presumably in the car or over his chair or maybe even at home, Hawkins talked to the employees about his vision of the new grocery store.

And these were real employees, as Penn Traffic took pains to point out in news accounts of the ads. The people nodding their heads, smiling, looking pleased with what they were hearing were actual employees of Penn Traffic. The ads prominently showed one woman crying, dabbing the corners of her eyes with a tissue. This transparent ploy prompted the *New Times*, the local alternative newsweekly and nobody's fool, to speculate that the tears had somehow been faked. But they were real enough. It's just that nobody imagined what kind of workplace, what levels of frustration, what history of indignities, might lead a person to cry during what amounts to a simple business meeting.

Of course, she could have been crying out of boredom. In one ad, Hawkins suggests that Penn Traffic will save lots of money with a more inexpensive kind of

bag and thus be able to pass that savings right along to the customers. In the audience, there are solemn nods all around. In another ad, Hawkins says the company will never again require shoppers to carry cards in order to receive a discount. Wide smiles. Did he really say *never*? In a third, Hawkins pulls out all the stops and decrees that no one will ever ask customers to present a receipt in order to make a return. The employees in the ads applaud politely, and the background music rises around them and then quickly fades as the grocery store's logo appears above the new motto: "All we did was listen."

Listen to whom? Now, nobody can seriously expect a commercial to show the chief executive listening to the cashier whose response to the survey described having to do price checks herself rather than ask for help. "I'm not being insensitive," she wrote, "but ... many employees lack reading skills. Rather than embarrass them I'll have to leave the register and do it myself." *There's* a set of problems that can't be addressed in thirty months, let alone thirty seconds. It was hard for me to watch the ads and not think about the responses I had read. One reasonable, seemingly simple request read in part:

We would like to receive our pay in actual checks rather than vouchers that must be cashed at the service desk. This is an archaic practice that most companies abandoned decades ago. My

AWFUL EXPLOSION OF COMMODORE STOCKTON'S GREAT GUN, THE "PEACEMAKER," ON BOARD THE U. S. STEAMSHIP PRINCETON.—1844.

The Secretaries of State and of the Navy, and Other Eminent Persons, Instantly Killed.—Miraculous Escape of the President.—Sudden Transition from the Height of Human Enjoyment to the Extreme of Woe.—Stockton's High Enthusiasm.—His Vast and Beautiful Ship.—Her Model and Armament. —Styled the Pride of the Navy.—Invitations for a Grand Gala Day.—President Tyler Attends.— Countless Dignitaries on Board.—Array of Female Beauty.—Music, Toasts, Wit and Wine.—Firing of the Monster Gun.—Its Perfect Success.—" One More Shot! " by Request.—A Stunning and Murderous Blast.—Bursting of the Gun.—Death all Around.—Frightful Shrieks and Groans —Scattering of Mangled Remains.—Agony of Woman's Heart.—Standing Place of the President.—Absent Just One Moment.—The Dead in Union Flags.—Funeral at the White House.

family and friends have a difficult time believing this is how I am paid, and I find it insulting to have my pay counted out in front of other employees, to say nothing of any customer who happens to be standing there. This is a private matter and should remain just that.

The listening that really mattered, though, was not that of some warm-hearted CEO, but ours in the audience. Even if Hawkins believed with all his heart in his Heart of the Matter seminars and his change exercises—and I suspect he did—ultimately the seminars were for the benefit of potential shoppers and investors. After all, news reports of Penn Traffic's near-death may have been widespread, but they weren't exaggerated. The doubters' minds needed easing. So the ads called together businessmen and businesswomen everywhere within hearing range of a TV and designated every single one of them an armchair CEO. Owners of stocks, mutual funds, and bonds, amateur investors, and even those who merely prick up their ears as the news anchors read the day's closings on stocks of local interest—all received engraved reservations for seats at the boardroom table and were invited guests at the company's meetings, because they understood, they knew about cost-cutting measures and savings. They were conversant in business and shared the culture's values.

INSTANTANEOUS

The conifer of forever
Stood tall in the forest.
Lumberjacks passed by
And took out their saws.

The stump was forever

The elephants of forever
Were shot down by poachers.
Their bodies were left to
Rot on the desert floor.

The tusks were forever

A hydroelectric dam
Was built across the river
Of forever. It created
Many jobs and much power.

The cost was forever

The protesters of forever
Demonstrated in the streets
They were tear gassed by
Police. Many were beaten.

The air and skin were forever

The car of forever
Pulled into a service station.
Employees and customers
Oohed and aahed.

The keys were forever

III

NOT THAT THE AD campaign helped Penn Traffic at all. In August 1998 the company held in excess of $1.4 billion in debt. Shares, which traded on the New York Stock

Tickets to the show
Of forever were on sale.
The night of the show
Ushers were at the gates.

The stubs were forever

A mugger assaulted
An unarmed pedestrian.
The man did not have
The money of forever.

The gun was forever

The lovers of forever
Looked at each other in bed.
They made love again.

The break up was forever

The author of forever
Signed ten thousand copies
Of his bestselling book.

The readers were forever

A dieter on the diet
Of forever stepped onto
The scale and looked down.

The number was forever

A shoplifter tripped
An alarm while leaving
The mall of forever.

The parking lot was forever

A poet who was working on
The work of forever
Wrote a poem of forevers.

The poem was over.

—David Hess

Exchange for $45 in 1993, now traded over-the-counter, often for less than a dollar and never for more than single-digits. After serving as CEO for one year and five months, Phil Hawkins abruptly resigned in August 1998. In November, the company hired Joseph Fisher. To commemorate the new beginning, Fisher struck an optimistic pose in the produce department of one of the grocery stores, and a newspaper photographer obligingly made it official. Even surrounded by bright red, green, and yellow vegetables, Fisher was the freshest, newest thing in the frame. Probably few readers of the newspaper recalled or even cared that just over a year before, Hawkins had posed for a nearly identical photograph. The produce department is a kind of coronation site for Penn Traffic CEOs fresh off the trucks and unpacked from their crates.

Not long after Fisher's ascension, a new television ad campaign began. "It's Gotta Be _____(fill in name of grocery store here)" is the new motto, eclipsing in the public's memory both "All We Did Is Listen" and the creepy previous slogan, "We Really Are Your Closest Friend." But curiously the corporate memory was also on the fritz. When I contacted company PR man Marc Jampole about taking a look at Penn Traffic's history over the last few years, beginning with that moment the company surveyed all its employees to get a sense of where it stood and what could be done to make the changes that needed changing and solve the problems that needed solving, he was less than enthusiastic about talking on those terms.

He did want to talk about Joseph Fisher, however; Fisher, I learned, was going to turn things at Penn Traffic around with his proven recipe of good merchandise, the right mix of sales and specials, and excellent customer service. "We won't discuss Phil," Jampole said. Months before he had refused my request for a videotape of the Hawkins TV ads. A week later I learned that Hawkins resigned, taking his motto, his seminars, and presumably his managing from the heart with him. When I pointed out that the survey I was curious about had actually been conducted and completed before the arrival of Hawkins, Jampole said that given all the "change and turmoil" Penn Traffic has gone through, it didn't make sense to look back that many years. "For us," said Jampole, "the beginning point is Joe Fisher."